Samuel French Acting Edition

Project Dawn

by Karen Hartman

SAMUELFRENCH.COM   SAMUELFRENCH.CO.UK

Copyright © 2019 by Karen Hartman
All Rights Reserved
Content drawn from *Power: A User's Manual* © 2018 by Vanessa Jackson,
Healing Circles, Inc.

PROJECT DAWN is fully protected under the copyright laws of the United States of America, the British Commonwealth, including Canada, and all other countries of the Copyright Union. All rights, including professional and amateur stage productions, recitation, lecturing, public reading, motion picture, radio broadcasting, television and the rights of translation into foreign languages are strictly reserved.

ISBN 978-0-573-70753-7

www.SamuelFrench.com
www.SamuelFrench.co.uk

FOR PRODUCTION ENQUIRIES

UNITED STATES AND CANADA
Info@SamuelFrench.com
1-866-598-8449

UNITED KINGDOM AND EUROPE
Plays@SamuelFrench.co.uk
020-7255-4302

Each title is subject to availability from Samuel French, depending upon country of performance. Please be aware that *PROJECT DAWN* may not be licensed by Samuel French in your territory. Professional and amateur producers should contact the nearest Samuel French office or licensing partner to verify availability.

CAUTION: Professional and amateur producers are hereby warned that *PROJECT DAWN* is subject to a licensing fee. Publication of this play(s) does not imply availability for performance. Both amateurs and professionals considering a production are strongly advised to apply to Samuel French before starting rehearsals, advertising, or booking a theatre. A licensing fee must be paid whether the title(s) is presented for charity or gain and whether or not admission is charged. Professional/Stock licensing fees are quoted upon application to Samuel French.

No one shall make any changes in this title(s) for the purpose of production. No part of this book may be reproduced, stored in a retrieval system, or transmitted in any form, by any means, now known or yet to be invented, including mechanical, electronic, photocopying, recording, videotaping, or otherwise, without the prior written permission of the publisher. No one shall upload this title(s), or part of this title(s), to any social media websites.

For all enquiries regarding motion picture, television, and other media rights, please contact Samuel French.

MUSIC USE NOTE

Licensees are solely responsible for obtaining formal written permission from copyright owners to use copyrighted music in the performance of this play and are strongly cautioned to do so. If no such permission is obtained by the licensee, then the licensee must use only original music that the licensee owns and controls. Licensees are solely responsible and liable for all music clearances and shall indemnify the copyright owners of the play(s) and their licensing agent, Samuel French, against any costs, expenses, losses and liabilities arising from the use of music by licensees. Please contact the appropriate music licensing authority in your territory for the rights to any incidental music.

IMPORTANT BILLING AND CREDIT REQUIREMENTS

If you have obtained performance rights to this title, please refer to your licensing agreement for important billing and credit requirements.

PROJECT DAWN was commissioned and produced by People's Light in Malvern, Pennsylvania as part of the New Play Frontiers Program (Executive Leaders: Abigail Adams, Ellen Anderson, and Zak Berkman).

PROJECT DAWN was first produced as a National New Play Network (nnpn.org) Rolling World Premiere by People's Light (Pennsylvania), Horizon Theatre (Georgia), and Unicorn Theatre (Missouri):

PROJECT DAWN opened at People's Light on June 14, 2017. The production was directed by Abigail Adams, with scenic and costume design by Jessica Ford, lighting design by Dennis Parichy, and sound design by Karin Graybash. The production stage manager was Audrey M. Brown. The cast was as follows:

NOELLE / ASHLEE	Claire Inie-Richards
RUTH / KRYSTAL	Melanye Finister
CASSIE / GWEN	Antoinette LaVecchia
JUDGE ROBERTA KAPLAN / BONNIE	Janis Dardaris
NIA / LOLA	Susanna Guzman
KYLA / SHONDELL	Yvette Ganier
SISTER CAROL / TRACY	Danielle Skraastad
BAILIFF VOICE	Nadira Beard

PROJECT DAWN opened at Horizon Theatre on September 29, 2017. The production was directed by Lisa Adler, with scenic design by Moriah Curley-Clay and Isabel Curley-Clay, lighting design by Mary Parker, costume design by Dr. L. Nyrobi Moss, and sound design by Kacie Willis. The production dramaturg was Maggie Markham, and the production stage manager was Julianna M. Lee. The cast was as follows:

NOELLE / ASHLEE	Brooke Owens
RUTH / KRYSTAL	Christy Clark
CASSIE / GWEN	Lane Carlock
JUDGE ROBERTA KAPLAN / BONNIE	Marianne Fraulo
NIA / LOLA	Maria Rodriguez-Sager
KYLA / SHONDELL	Bobbi Lynne Scott
SISTER CAROL / TRACY	Carolyn Cook
BAILIFF VOICE	Tempest D. Armstrong

PROJECT DAWN opened at Unicorn Theatre on January 27, 2018. The production was directed by Heidi Van, with scenic design by Emily Swenson, lighting design by Art Kent, costume design by Georgianna Londré Buchanan, and sound design by David Kiehl. The production dramaturg was Mary Allison Joseph, and the production stage manager was Tanya Brown. The cast was as follows:

NOELLE / ASHLEE	Leah Swank-Miller
RUTH / KRYSTAL	Lanette King
CASSIE / GWEN	Jennifer Mays
JUDGE ROBERTA KAPLAN / BONNIE	Kathleen Warfel
NIA / LOLA	Vanessa A. Davis
KYLA / SHONDELL	Nedra Dixon
SISTER CAROL / TRACY	Amy Elizabeth Attaway

The action of *Project Dawn* takes place during five monthly sessions of Project Dawn Court, an alternative treatment court in Philadelphia for women with multiple prostitution convictions.

The women plead guilty before they begin in the court, so the facts are not in dispute. Thus the defense attorney and the public defender mostly work together.

If a woman successfully completes the program (drug counseling, trauma therapy, monthly court appearances, and weekly parole meetings) her charges are dropped. If she fails at the program, she does time.

CHARACTERS

Seven women each play a participant and a staff member in the court.
In speaking order:

ACTOR 1
(White, early twenties)

ASHLEE – Sullen, almost catatonic.

NOELLE – A fresh-faced intern and aspiring lawyer.

ACTOR 2
(Black, thirties or forties)

KRYSTAL – Wears an Islamic veil sometimes. She's chatty.

RUTH – Senior therapist for the program, Christian but works in many modalities.

ACTOR 3
(White, forties)

CASSIE – (thirties) Has a hip injury, uses a cane.

GWEN – (forties) The public defender who co-founded the program with Kyla. Open hearted, sharp-witted mother of four, on overload.

ACTOR 4
(White, fifties or sixties)

BONNIE – A graduate of the program, now a motivational speaker.

JUDGE ROBERTA KAPLAN – Compassionate, patient, and focused. An old-school Jewish liberal, Philadelphia style, which means she blends with Quakers.

ACTOR 5
(Latina, thirties or forties)

LOLA – Curvy, sweet, may speak with a slight accent.

NIA [NEE uh] – The hyper-competent court coordinator, excellent rapport with staff and participants. The other staff address her as a peer, not an assistant.

ACTOR 6
(Black, forties)

SHONDELL – A grandma. She wears an eyepatch or bandage.

KYLA – The DA or prosecuting attorney, a quicksilver legal mind. A butch woman, sometimes mistaken for male in off-hours.

ACTOR 7
(White, forty-ish)

TRACY – (forty-ish) Bleached hair, tattoos. Ran a major drug cartel, has a swagger the other women lack.

SISTER CAROL – (eighty) Activist nun who founded and runs May's Place, a residence for former prostitutes. Full of righteous rage. Sister Carol is not a court regular, therefore Tracy becomes an anchor among the court clients.

We also hear the voice of an African-American female **BAILIFF**. Her voice surrounds us, rather than coming from one source. OR the Bailiff can be cast live. A substantial presence, age flexible.

Everyone except Lola and Noelle grew up in Philadelphia. The Philly dialect is specific and worth a listen.

SETTING

A worn but functional courtroom on the eleventh floor
of a municipal building.
It is always the wrong temperature in this room.

TIME

December 2013 – March 2014

AUTHOR'S NOTES

Clothes and Bodies

Most actors shift roles on a dime with little or no costume change, i.e. Ashlee sheds a baggy coat and cap to reveal Noelle, Krystal drops her hijab to a scarf and adds a blazer as Ruth. The Judge wears court robes and makes a full change to Bonnie. Tracy can be more defined in a court client look and make a full change to Sister Carol. A range of body types would be ideal. Some character shifts noted in the script follow director Abigail Adams' original staging; there may be other ways to do it.

Sidebars

In sidebar, the staff speak off the record and away from the clients. It could be just a light shift or include a physical move to the judge's bench. The staff shows more personality in sidebar. However, they are also very different from one another and everyone defers to the Judge. So it isn't exactly relaxed.

Staging and Tone

We probably view the court from Judge Kaplan's perspective, looking at the spectator seats of the courtroom upstage and defense and prosecution tables downstage. The placement of audience is flexible, as long as the Judge can see the whole courtroom – nothing happens behind her back.

Gwen and Noelle sit at the defense table. Kyla sits at the prosecution table. Ruth could sit in the front row and stand with her clients. Nia works a landline phone, boxes of files, and an ancient computer from a card table in the jury box. The court participants sit in the spectator section unless someone has violated a rule, in which case she sits near Nia in the jury box, where she can be more closely supervised.

The tone is bright. Time is always of the essence, and the action moves with urgency, but each case is important, and the staff gives each participant her moment of full attention. The staff is on-mission, except for the Bailiff, who is so over it.

Punctuation

Overlapping text is indicated by a slash (/) where the next speech begins.

Thanks

Project Dawn was researched over a year of observation and interviews with staff and participants from Dawn's Place and the Philadelphia Project Dawn Court between fall 2013 and fall 2014, as well as interviews with other community supporters.

All characters are fictional. Particularly with regard to the staff, drama has been invented in cases where the author met calm, kind, deeply sane individuals.

Deep gratitude to the following individuals and institutions who conducted or supported interviews. Your generosity made this work possible:

Marcie Bramucci • Jeannette Cole • Natalie Dallard, LCSW • Dawn's Place • Mary DeFusco, Esq. • Senator Andy Dinniman • Arielle Egan • Sara Gruen • Sister Teresita Hinnegan • Vanessa Jackson, LCSW • The Johnson House • Anne Marie Jones • Sandy Kornhauser • Sister Michelle Loisel, DC • Regina Marshall • Carol Hart Metzker • Brendale McAfee • Linda Muraresku • Hon. Judge Marsha Neifield • Donna Price • Project Dawn Court • Shea M. Rhodes, Esquire • Derek Riker • Lesha Sanders • Christina Sappey • Corey Shdaimah • Sister Terry Shields • Vern Thiessen • Sister Eileen White

Note on Casting

In university and school productions only, *Project Dawn* may be performed by fourteen actors instead of doubling. In that case, the roles of Noelle, Cassie, Gwen, Judge Kaplan, Nia, Tracy, and Sister Carol may be cast as performers of any race. All other roles are racially specified in the dialogue and need to stay as they are.

ACT ONE

(As lights shift, the Project Dawn Court staff assembles: Public defender **GWEN** *and intern* **NOELLE** *sit at the defense table. DA* **KYLA** *sits at the prosecution table. Senior therapist* **RUTH** *sits in the front row of spectators. From a card table in the jury box, court coordinator* **NIA** *works a landline phone, boxes of files, and an ancient computer.* **JUDGE KAPLAN** *sits elevated at her bench. A small battalion, poised to serve.)*

(Hold. Actors transform into the Project Dawn Court Clients: **CASSIE**, **ASHLEE**, **SHONDELL**, **KRYSTAL**, *and* **LOLA**, *adding* **TRACY** *[*JUDGE *remains herself here]. Equally strong and alert but more ragged and variously defiant and afraid.)*

(Blackout.)

(A ladies' room on the eleventh floor of the Philadelphia Criminal Justice building. As you might imagine, no frills.)

*(***KRYSTAL*** wears cheap, bright clothes and a hijab. She tells a funny story on her cell phone, casual and loud. She relates a fun discovery with zero self-pity:)*

KRYSTAL. Yeah you know him down the street on East Archer Avenue? The chubby one. Naw, naw, naw the *light*-skinneded chubby one. Wait for it...he *molested* me!

(Call isn't clear. She tries the punchline again:)

He *molested* me!

(ASHLEE approaches KRYSTAL. Hair in her eyes. Monotone to the point of catatonic:)

ASHLEE. I need a smoke.

KRYSTAL. *(To ASHLEE.)* It's my *sister*.

ASHLEE. I gave you smokes; now I need one.

KRYSTAL. *(On the phone, ignoring ASHLEE, still a funny story.)* Yeah, yeah it started after the twins came! He gave me candy. Don't you remember the candy? Didn't I share that candy? You liked that candy.

Well he never penetrated me for a while. He would just put my hand on his penis, put my mouth on his penis, little stuff like that.

ASHLEE. I know you got them.

KRYSTAL. Trust me if those twins hadn't been born no one woulda had a chance to molest me. Mommy was paying *attention* before them.

   (Listens.)

Naw you were at *school*.

   (Listens.)

Naw naw naw I *suppressed* it!

ASHLEE. It's almost nine; they're starting court.

KRYSTAL. This is a intimate conversation. Do you mind?

ASHLEE. Yeah I mind. I heard this shit in group.

KRYSTAL. *(On phone.)* All these years...what is it thirty forty years? Trust me, when it came to the front of my mind I about threw up in my own lap. Changes my story I tell you that.

   (ASHLEE gets up close to KRYSTAL, who fishes through her bag and hands ASHLEE a tampon.)

I have a lot of flashbacks about the penetration. A *lot*. Remember in college I started hearing voices? You never know what you got up in your brain.

I recommend the therapeutic process, it is educational. Girl, you don't have to be arrested to try it.

ASHLEE. This is a tampon.

KRYSTAL. Huh? What do you mean? How you know where he is?

ASHLEE. I don't need a tampon. I need a cigarette.

KRYSTAL. Why would I look him up?

I don't care how much money he has now.

Why would I care how much money he has?

> (**ASHLEE** *listens, not without compassion.*)

He's not my type.

> *(Pause.)*

He's not my type.

> *(Pause.)*

He wasn't my type when I was four; he ain't my type now.

> *(A testy* **BAILIFF'S VOICE** *brings us into the play. Even if the* **BAILIFF** *is live, these initial two-word announcements of court will probably be recorded, for flow.)*

BAILIFF'S VOICE. December court.

> *(During the* **BAILIFF**'s *announcement, the Project Dawn Court staff and participants assemble:* **GWEN** *sits at the defense table,* **KYLA** *sits at the prosecution table.* **KRYSTAL** *transforms into* **RUTH** *and takes her seat with staff.* **ASHLEE**, **LOLA**, *and* **TRACY** *sit in the spectator part of the courtroom with other participants we don't see.)*

> *(The* **BAILIFF**'s *announcement is the theater's cell phone announcement, if possible.)*

Court is now in session. December 9. There is no eating in the courtroom. There are no cell phones in the courtroom unless you have permission from the court to use them, which you don't. Your presence is court mandated and you will stay all day through all status reports so as to benefit from one another's experiences

and wisdom. Do not leave the floor without a subpoena for your next date. No texting. No selfies. No gum.
The Honorable Judge Roberta Kaplan presiding. All rise.

> *(All rise. **JUDGE KAPLAN** enters. She sits at the bench, then everyone sits. The **JUDGE** stays seated during court. **JUDGE**'s gavel.)*

Violations number sixty-seven and seventy-three, Miss Lola Vargas.

> *(**LOLA** gets to the front of the courtroom.)*
>
> *(**GWEN** stands with **LOLA**.)*

GWEN. Your Honor this is Ms. Lola Vargas. Ms. Vargas attends Chances recovery program and lives with her sister and the sister's boyfriend. Ms. Vargas understands this is not a perfect arrangement and she's been studying for her GED while holding down her job at McDonald's. Lola has attended all group and individual therapy sessions with Ruth this month, all check-ins with me, and two supervised visits with her daughter. Her goal is to reunite with her child in independent housing.

JUDGE. Thank you, Counsel.

GWEN. Thank you, Your Honor.

JUDGE. Ms. Vargas, anything to add?

LOLA. I'm doing good. Seeing my daughter for longer.

JUDGE. How is she?

LOLA. Bad and whiny.

JUDGE. That means she needs you.

> *(**LOLA** nods cheerfully.)*

LOLA. I'm motivated, Your Honor! I want my rights back!

JUDGE. Good. Ruth? Any report from therapy?

RUTH. Lola is still quiet in group.

LOLA. I *listen*.

RUTH. Lola listens. But Lola needs to speak up for Lola.

GWEN. People take advantage of her.

LOLA. Your Honor I know I'm never going back out there. My boys grew up without me but Ana is young, I can be there for her.

JUDGE. Wonderful.

LOLA. I used to say if I could get high with no consequences I'd never stop getting high but that's not true today. I'm clear-minded. When I make a decision it's coming from my right mind. It's not distorted because I'm high. You know what I mean?

(**TRACY** *whoops her support. Others may join.*)

JUDGE. Good. Ms. Grant?

KYLA. The district attorney is seeing what we want to see from Ms. Vargas in phase two. She is taking responsibility for her studies, her job, her daughter. I'm not hearing excuses. I like this report.

LOLA. Thank you!

GWEN. Your Honor, Ms. Vargas has a request.

LOLA. You ask.

GWEN. You can ask for what you need.

LOLA. Your Honor, my mother called me? She's living all the way in California? I never heard from her in twenty years. She wants to buy me a ticket to visit.

KYLA. Your Honor, Ms. Vargas would need written permission to leave the state.

JUDGE. I need to go through your record and think about that.

LOLA. I am committed, Your Honor.

JUDGE. Glad to hear it. How about the diabetes?

LOLA. What?

JUDGE. Are you monitoring your sugar levels?

LOLA. Yeah but no.

JUDGE. What happened?

LOLA. I met with the nutritionist, but I couldn't go with the menu she gave me.

JUDGE. You need to tell her it doesn't work for you.

LOLA. I should do it I know, I just... I'm not gonna eat that. So I just say thank you, I'll do it.

JUDGE. You need to *tell* her you're going to cheat, and maybe she'll come up with something that's not quite as good as perfect but not as bad as what you would do on your own.

LOLA. Thank you Your Honor. I'll do that.

JUDGE. Huh. May I see everyone at sidebar please?

> *(Sidebar. The staff [* **JUDGE KAPLAN**, **GWEN**, **RUTH**, **KYLA** *] cluster privately to speak off the record. Time pressure abides, despite digressions.)*

Ruth, I'd like you to read Kim's letter.

RUTH. Your Honor?

JUDGE. It would be instructive for Lola.

KYLA. I agree with Judge Kaplan. What if Lola loses her foot or her eyesight? She needs to take care of the health piece or she'll spiral back down.

RUTH. That's some very heavy news, right before Christmas.

JUDGE. You and Kim were close.

RUTH. I spent more time talking to Kim last year than to my husband.

GWEN. You talk to your husband?

RUTH. Your Honor, I recognize Kim had poor health habits, but sweet Lord I eat Dunkin' Donuts every day.

GWEN. And I see you there.

> *(High five* **GWEN** *and* **RUTH***?)*

With respect Your Honor this is a court, not Weight Watchers. I'd like to live healthy too. Walk ten thousand steps, cook for my kids, sleep six hours, but you know what? Tough.

KYLA. Self care –

GWEN. The *jargon*.

KYLA. The Lord says, "Caring for myself is an act of survival." And by Lorde I mean Audre Lorde.

JUDGE. *(Good-natured.)* I know who you mean.

GWEN. Your Honor there is a difference between too many Snickers and sex-for-smack, and if we police diet *no one* will graduate this program, we will *never* have clout for the full-time lawyer City Hall *promised would replace me three years ago*, and one day you'll find me under the covers at noon with a bottle of Percocet and a Beyoncé video.

RUTH. That's my kind of party.

GWEN. You're invited. You too Kyla, but don't bring us your kale.

RUTH. We can't all be vegans.

KYLA. Actually we can.

These girls have criminal convictions. They owe time. Project Dawn Court is a girl's last chance; to avoid jail she has to work the program. And medical care, including nutrition, is part of the program.

(ASHLEE is suddenly the intern NOELLE.)

NOELLE. I make oatmeal!

(Everyone looks at NOELLE.)

In a mug! With flax!

KYLA. What are these words?

GWEN. Noelle is my new intern. From Seattle.

NOELLE. Hi! Gwen if you prefer oatmeal I can make it for you in court; it won't take any longer than stopping for donuts. I just need hot water. I'll look around for outlets.

RUTH. Child?

NOELLE. I could make oatmeal for the clients too. Fifty bowls would cost maybe twenty-five bucks and that's with raisins and sugar.

LOLA. Should I sit down or are you still talking about me?

JUDGE. Excuse us, Lola, we're discussing procedure.

LOLA. Okay I'll just stand here.

(GWEN and NOELLE sit at Gwen's table.)

RUTH. *(Low voice re:* **NOELLE,** *to* **KYLA.***)* What happened to her last girl?

KYLA. The Weeper?

RUTH. Yeah her.

KYLA. "Oh those poor whores it's just too sad for me to be here. Me me me me me."

JUDGE. Ruth?

RUTH. I'll read the letter, Your Honor.

> *(The* **JUDGE** *hits her gavel. The lights shift back.)*

BAILIFF'S VOICE. Court is back in session. Get that phone away, Miss Paladino. Final warning.

TRACY. I was taking notes on the wisdom.

JUDGE. Ruth has a card from Kim who as many of you know had reached phase four of the program and was due to graduate next month. Kim was hospitalized, and hoped to come in person to tell you all how much you meant to her. Unfortunately, she won't have that opportunity. Kim died Thursday of kidney failure.

> *(***LOLA** *gasps. Others too. Everyone loved Kim.)*

Ruth?

RUTH. Kim died clean. She was able to make amends to her sister. Her little boy crawled into her hospital bed. Kim achieved dignity, and the love and forgiveness of her family. Here are her words:

> *(As* **RUTH** *reads,* **LOLA** *becomes upset.* **RUTH** *is upset too but controls it.)*

"Dear Project Dawn Court Girls, I want to thank you for being there for me in proud times and shameful times. I wish I had more years to enjoy life with the help of my God and my friends. Because of you and this Court, my sons knew me. Not Addict Kim, but the real Kim hiding under the drugs and the life. I call her Shiny Kim. I want more time and I hope we will have more time.

Thank you especially to Ruth" – we can skip this part.

JUDGE. Read it Ruth.

RUTH. "Ruth never looked at me with scorn or with fear. From day one, she saw me as a child of God."

(As herself.) Of course in a public program we did not use religious terms.

(Back to the letter.) "For the miracle of Project Dawn, I thank my Higher Power who Ruth and I call Jesus Christ.

Work hard and make good choices. This life is one short sip of water. Yours forever, Kim."

> *(Pause.)*

JUDGE. Don't yes me Lola.

Don't yes the nutritionist.

Find a way to take care of yourself that is real.

LOLA. Yes Your Honor.

JUDGE. Get your holiday bag from Nia.

LOLA. Merry Christmas Judge Kaplan.

JUDGE. Thank you Lola.

> *(**LOLA** sits at Nia's table. **NOELLE** moves to the client area, becomes **ASHLEE**.)*

BAILIFF'S VOICE. Numbers twenty-three, forty-seven, and eighty-four. Tracy Palladino.

> *(**TRACY** stands. **GWEN** rises with **TRACY**.)*

GWEN. Your Honor, this is Ms. Tracy Palladino. Tracy has completed her phase two of the program and enters phase three of four.

> *(Whoops from the other clients.)*

We are proud of Tracy. She already had her GED and has been taking courses in accounting, computer programming, and –

TRACY. New media.

GWEN. There you go. Maybe Tracy will soon put her considerable intelligence to positive use.

JUDGE. I look forward to that day.

GWEN. Tracy is in residence at May's Place but her stay there is set to expire in two months so she is investigating options.

JUDGE. How is May's Place?

TRACY. If you'da told me I'd live with a bunch of nuns and like it, I'da told you to give me some of what you're smoking. But I do. I live with a bunch of nuns and I love it. Sister Carol encourages worship is the only thing and I'm not too familiar with worship but Gwen has been taking me to church and to her home for Sunday brunch.

JUDGE. That's kind of you, Gwen.

GWEN. It puts my kids on better behavior having company.

TRACY. Works for me.

JUDGE. Ms. Grant?

KYLA. I have no trouble with Ms. Palladino this month.

JUDGE. Good work. I'll see you in January.

>   (**TRACY** *clears her throat, looking at* **GWEN**: *What about the thing?*)

GWEN. Your Honor, Tracy is seeking help with a legal muddle. I've looked into it but my hours are limited, while I'm waiting for that permanently funded full-time hire.

JUDGE. Go ahead, Tracy.

TRACY. Your Honor, my sister who's raising my son? I have the best family. I mean I have the best family. They stood by me through – through everything I done, I mean my sister she's *raising my son* and I can't even give her money no more, now that I'm clean.

But when my sister was in Iraq and I was doing all the bad things I did, I did some of it in her name.

JUDGE. I don't follow.

GWEN. Her ID.

JUDGE. Ah.

TRACY. Her license is dirty. Because of me. And I need a way to clear that up. I *need* to clear that up.

After everything I took from society... She's in *Iraq* up against *Saddamn* and I used her license. I wasn't myself at that time. I didn't care. I got what I wanted when I wanted. I was making seven grand a day.

ASHLEE. Shit.

GWEN. Tracy leave that part out.

TRACY. I'm not bragging.

(She is bragging.)

I was in a different business from these other girls, that's all.

KYLA. Ms. Palladino is fortunate to be in this treatment court and not upstate with the dealers on her level.

TRACY. I know! I'm a lucky person. Without incriminating myself: I'm the luckiest person in this court.

KYLA. We weighed your record very carefully in choosing to admit you to the Project Dawn Court. It was not unanimous.

TRACY. I am naturally fortunate. That was part of the secret to my success. I was very successful but it still wasn't enough for my habit, so how successful was I, you know what I'm saying? If I'm going to blow through all that money every night and still be on the street hustling by four a.m., that's not really success. And I believe in success. This is America!

JUDGE. It is America.

TRACY. This program has helped me so much. Thing is I did what I did as *her*. But *she* is a good person whereas I've been mostly a negative.

JUDGE. You're fortunate to have a supportive family.

TRACY. I talk to my sister every day. She calls me every *day*.

JUDGE. That's extraordinary.

TRACY. She's got my son, and she's driving him around without a license, living under the table with that stress and that risk because of *me*. Dylan's doing great, he's a little badass excuse me. She's got him in martial arts, everything.

KYLA. That'll serve him well.

TRACY. My sister knows where to put the rage. I never understood that until you ladies.

KYLA. Thus the armed robbery?

TRACY. *(Quick.)* I was in the back of the car.

Now my sister can't even claim all her vet bennies because her ID comes up dirty. I can't have *my* shit on *her* head.

JUDGE. Nia?

(LOLA has become NIA, the court coordinator.)

NIA. Apparently the sister has to go through...because they do look alike so the sister has to prove that her name is no longer Tracy's alias. It's beyond the DMV. It's into fraud inspection, the Narcotics Bureau, Homeland Security because of the international origin of the drugs. Tracy had a wide reach.

TRACY. I was good. But I was good in a bad way.

GWEN. It's more than I can get into, Your Honor, in my spare time. Of course once the mayor funds a full-time Project Dawn lawyer, the court will have ample resources –

TRACY. I coulda funded ten lawyers a *day*. I'm serious. I could be running May's Place and paying the nuns so we wouldn't have to pool our food stamps. And once my body art brand goes viral I will donate to those less fortunate girls.

I won't donate my art though. I do that for the money.

(She shows off a tattoo.)

"Star Marks: Be the One That Shines."

JUDGE. Nia?

NIA. Holding with Narcotics.

GWEN. Can we streamline the ID process so that once Narcotics clears, the sister's name is clean in the database?

NIA. On it.

TRACY. How long will that take? She could get pulled over any day. She's a saint, but still.

JUDGE. Your sister has stood by you this far; she is probably not going to give up over the license. For now keep working the program, stay on track so that you graduate in April.

TRACY. I'm going clean for her.

JUDGE. *(For the group.)* Ladies, this is a selfish program. You have to do it for yourself. The second you say I'm doing this for my kids, or for my sister, and that person disappoints you, you have an excuse to use. Tracy is lucky to still have support, after the choices she made.

TRACY. *(Also for the group.)* I was choosing choices that were mostly wrong. All wrong.

I apologize for taking more than my share of time.

JUDGE. Okay, see you at our next full court, is that January 12?

BAILIFF'S VOICE. Palladino. Subpoena for January 12.

> *(**TRACY** sits down.)*

Numbers twenty-seven, twenty-eight, thirty-one, and sixty-four. Krystal Williams.

> *(**KRYSTAL** comes to the front of the court. She has added a face veil. **ASHLEE** becomes **NOELLE**.)*

GWEN. Your Honor this is Ms. Krystal Williams. She attends IOP at Step Ahead Recovery. She's been on time to her appointments, clean urines. She has been living with an uncle, is that right?

KRYSTAL. Yes ma'am.

JUDGE. Does the court have an address?

KRYSTAL. Skyline Homes.

NIA. Seventh and West Erie?

KRYSTAL. That's right.

GWEN. Krystal completed her thirty meetings in thirty days sanction.

(Applause.)

JUDGE. How was that?

KRYSTAL. It was useful, Your Honor. I like the structure.

JUDGE. Pardon me, I can't hear you clearly.

*(**KRYSTAL** drops the veil from her face.)*

KRYSTAL. I like the structure.

JUDGE. Thank you. That's better.

KRYSTAL. With a structure you can find your path. The dangerous thing for me is my thoughts. The thoughts used to go some pretty bad places but I am here with gratitude.

Ruth says faith can get a person through some deep water.

JUDGE. Does she?

KRYSTAL. *(To **KYLA**.)* Did you know black people have mental illness?

KYLA. I did know that, yes.

KRYSTAL. We have some things to learn as a culture, right? Like how to get rich off other people obviously, but also more awareness of trauma, psychosis, medication, things like that.

KYLA. I'm glad you completed your thirty in thirty. Takes discipline to work a program.

KRYSTAL. What I see now, what I know now, that's what's up.

JUDGE. See you next month. January 12.

*(**KRYSTAL** grins.)*

KRYSTAL. Yes Your Honor!

JUDGE. Feels good to come in doing what you were supposed to do?

KRYSTAL. Feels great Your Honor.

BAILIFF'S VOICE. Williams, January 12.

*(**KRYSTAL** sits down.)*

(The day passes. Could be as simple as a light shift and a series of gavels. This court goes on forever with no breaks and no lunch.)

JUDGE. Those are all the summary judgments, correct?

GWEN. Thirty-eight clients, Your Honor.

NOELLE. Big day.

GWEN. Medium day.

KYLA. We have the no-shows.

JUDGE. What's the list.

(Quickly, procedure:)

KYLA. Helen Marcos.

NIA. She called, she has a cold and a sinus infection, she can accept service elsewhere on another date.

KYLA. Laurie Mahoney.

NIA. No contact.

KYLA. I request a bench warrant, Your Honor.

GWEN. I agree.

JUDGE. Bench warrant.

KYLA. Regina Smith. She missed the last status update.

GWEN. I haven't seen Regina in three weeks. I'm concerned.

NIA. *(From phone.)* Dignity House had a check-in last night. Regina's on day forty-one of her sixty-day stay.

NOELLE. How did you know to call them?

JUDGE. Good. Give her a two-week date and let's see what's going on.

KYLA. That's all I've got.

JUDGE. So that brings us to Cassie.

KYLA. Yes. Cassie.

*(**GWEN** becomes **CASSIE**, who has been sitting all day in the jury box near Nia.)*

BAILIFF'S VOICE. Ms. Cassandra MacMillan. Violations twenty-one, forty-four, fifty-seven, forty-nine, and sixty.

*(**CASSIE** makes her way to the front of the court, limping badly.)*

RUTH. Your Honor, this is Cassie MacMillan.

JUDGE. Do you know why you've been in the jury box all day, Ms. MacMillan?

CASSIE. I had a positive urine. From a prescription for Percocet. For my *hip*.

KYLA. Your Honor we got a hot urine back yesterday, showing painkillers prescribed and unprescribed, as well as amphetamines, and heroin.

CASSIE. Relapse is part of recovery.

KYLA. This is your third.

CASSIE. I'm here ain't I? I don't come to court when I get high, I run. I'm not running. I changed. Because I need my surgery.

JUDGE. We are glad you are here. What happened?

CASSIE. There was a fire at Gaudenzia House on Friday night.

I called my mom –

> *(She sobs. She is in real physical and psychic pain, and also performing. Okay for this to feel ugly.)*

– and I said Mom can I come up to you, and she said, you're an adult.

That rejection made it okay in my mind to use. There was nowhere for me to go.

RUTH. Your Honor – Cassie described it as a severe case of the eff-its.

JUDGE. I see.

CASSIE. *(Weeping.)* I have nowhere to live. No income. Step Up House wants to see income. I got to have my surgery or I can't walk, I can't work.

JUDGE. What's the recovery time for your surgery?

CASSIE. I don't know.

JUDGE. Where are you planning to stay after your surgery?

CASSIE. I don't know.

JUDGE. Nia?

NIA. On hold with SSI.

(To **CASSIE.***)* Due to your disability we can try to move you up my list more quickly.

CASSIE. When I get my surgery I won't be disabled no more.

NIA. So let's get you housed now.

JUDGE. Where are you living?

CASSIE. I'm staying in Simple Homes with some friends. I watch their little girl and give them my food stamps.

JUDGE. Not a situation for when you leave the hospital and require care.

CASSIE. I need help.

JUDGE. Ms. Grant?

KYLA. Your Honor as noted this is the third relapse. Ms. MacMillan had a usage before the November court so we're not even looking at thirty days clean. We have exhausted sanctions and community service and I recommend custody.

*(***CASSIE*** flat out bawls.)*

CASSIE. How am I going to get my surgery? My hip hurts so bad.

JUDGE. Sidebar.

(Sidebar light. **CASSIE** *flips on a dime into* **GWEN.***)*

GWEN. Your Honor, my client is in crushing physical pain. She finally has the surgery set, she has a dental pull set. She would like to remain at Gaudenzia but they require proof of income.

NIA. I got an appointment for her at Social Services to update her housing requirements.

GWEN. She has an intake for pre-surgery tomorrow, Your Honor.

JUDGE. Kyla?

KYLA. She is using, she is on the Avenue, and she is going to die. Could Cassie have the surgery in jail?

NIA. *(On phone.)* County's telling me hip surgery is too specialized for their medical unit. It's the hospital or nothing.

NOELLE. How do you know what to do before they tell you what to do?

NIA. I have a lot of degrees and I pay attention.

NOELLE. How come you're not a lawyer?

NIA. I dislike assholes.

> *(**JUDGE**'s gavel. End of sidebar. Back to **CASSIE**.)*

JUDGE. Cassie. Do you have an appointment book?

CASSIE. I lost it Your Honor. But I have a killer memory.

JUDGE. Against the district attorney's recommendation, and perhaps against my better judgment, I am not going to put you into custody. Only because you have a surgery scheduled and I don't want to send you to the back of the list.

CASSIE. Thank you Your Honor!

JUDGE. Nia will write out your appointments. Doctors, the dentist, group and individual with Ruth, the SSI meeting. You must get each appointment slip signed by the person you meet with, *and* call Nia after every one. If you miss an appointment, if you are *late* to an appointment, you go to jail. We're out of choices.

CASSIE. I'm going to be so perfect, and I'm going to get my hip fixed up so I can work!

JUDGE. Good. Two weeks, that's?

BAILIFF'S VOICE. December 22.

JUDGE. Sit with Nia.

CASSIE. Okay.

JUDGE. And we are closed.

> *(She strikes her gavel.)*

BAILIFF'S VOICE. Next date, January 12.

> (**NOELLE**, *wearing heels that would be adorable in another context, loads heavy cardboard boxes of files onto a dolly.*)
>
> (**CASSIE** *goes over to Nia's desk and sits down, weeping.* **NIA** *gives her tissues.*)

NIA. I'm going to write it all out for you and here's the box where they sign that you showed up, got it?

CASSIE. My hip hurts so bad.

NIA. I know baby.

CASSIE. And I'm bleeding like a stuck pig.

> (**NIA** *pulls a box of tampons out of her own purse.* **CASSIE** *takes the whole box without acknowledgment.*)

NIA. *(Setting a boundary.)* Take what you need.

> (**CASSIE** *grabs a bunch and gives the box back.*)

CASSIE. Thanks.

NIA. After your surgery we'll do the shopping closet, okay?

CASSIE. Save me some sparkly clothes.

NIA. With bling.

CASSIE. You're really nice.

NIA. You have to call after every appointment.

CASSIE. I won't miss a single one.

NIA. But you also have to call. The judge will come down on you next time.

CASSIE. You're good at your job and you're nice.

NIA. That's a kind thing to say.

> (**CASSIE** *limps out of the room with her paper.* **NOELLE** *watches* **CASSIE**, *moved.*)

Go in the bathroom to cry.

NOELLE. I'm not gonna cry.

NIA. The last girl cried and now she's watching Netflix on her mama's couch.

NOELLE. I'm not gonna cry.

NIA. Pretend you have to throw up. Go right now.

> (**NOELLE** *takes a deep breath in and holds it. Exhales. She's weirdly fine.*)

NOELLE. I'm in control.

NIA. Did Gwen mention secondary trauma?

NOELLE. She just said can you get on a plane Monday, court's Tuesday.

NIA. You flew to Philly for this? Yesterday?

NOELLE. Gwen gave a talk at my school and –

NIA. Got it.

NOELLE. What happened to Cassie's hip?

NIA. Bad rape.

NOELLE. What's in the bag?

NIA. Shopping closet. We all collect. Girls pick out what they want in the side room before court. A little spooky, first time you see a participant in your clothes.

NOELLE. I want to be part of the solution!

NIA. I'm gonna go get shitfaced with some girls from fourth floor. Wanna come?

NOELLE. I need to get these files back to Gwen.

NIA. After?

NOELLE. Yeah. No, yeah. Definitely!

> (**NIA** *goes, lugging her bags of donated clothing.* **GWEN** *enters in winter boots, on a call.*)

GWEN. Thank you Doctor, my daughter is fortunate to be working with you. I'll keep those suggestions in mind.

> *(Ends call.)*

(To **NOELLE***.)* Where's your boots?

NOELLE. Hi Gwen! You're still here! I didn't bring them.

GWEN. Who you trying to impress?

NOELLE. You?

GWEN. Good. But I'm straight. So bring boots. Dogshit slush out there.

NOELLE. I knew we dressed up for court, I didn't understand the whole...

GWEN. You get pneumonia I'm fucked.

NOELLE. *(Hearing the compliment.)* Thanks.

GWEN. And if you're on medication, stay on it.

NOELLE. I'm not?

GWEN. What is up with these kids and anxiety disorder? What the fuck?

NOELLE. It's really common.

GWEN. Anxiety disorder? What even is that?

NOELLE. It's persistent worry over six or more months out of proportion to cause.

GWEN. Yes but what the fuck *is* it? What is going on?

NOELLE. I don't know how to answer that?

GWEN. Do you have an anxiety disorder?

NOELLE. No.

GWEN. Are you depressed?

NOELLE. No.

GWEN. Are you out of touch with reality in any way?

NOELLE. Only in the sense that I believe in positive change.

*(**GWEN** scans her, skeptical.)*

GWEN. Fuck it. You'll crack or you won't. I gotta get to Muncy.

*(**NOELLE** hands her a bag, checks from a list.)*

NOELLE. Here's Kathleen's file, emergency contact info, maps if the GPS goes out, your overnight bag just in case.

GWEN. Good. Any questions?

NOELLE. Yes.

GWEN. Hold 'em.

(She exits.)

(Loud house music. **NIA** and **NOELLE** drink shots and dance.)*

NOELLE. SO YOU KNOW THE WOMEN, OR GIRLS, OR... WHY DO WE CALL THEM GIRLS?

NIA. WHAT'S YOUR POINT?

NOELLE. WE'RE ALL, "MAKE GOOD CHOICES," BUT AREN'T THEY MENTALLY UNSTABLE?

NIA. THEY'RE MEDICATED, YEAH.

NOELLE. WELL?

NIA. FOR PTSD. IT DOESN'T MEAN THEY'RE CRAZY.

NOELLE. THEY GO TO THERAPY?

NIA. HELL YES, EVERY WEEK WITH RUTH, GROUP AND INDIVIDUAL.

NOELLE. BUT WE'RE SAYING LIFE IS PRECIOUS, YOUR LIFE IS THIS GLASS EGG TO CARRY AROUND WITHOUT BREAKING IT, OR SOMETHING, LIKE HOW WE GREW UP: LIFE IS PRECIOUS, CHOICES MATTER, ALL THAT?

NIA. YOU DON'T KNOW HOW I GREW UP.

NOELLE. YOU SAID YOU HAVE A LOT OF DEGREES.

NIA. YES I DO.

NOELLE. WHAT IF THEIR LIVES ARE NOT PRECIOUS? WHAT IF THEIR LIVES ARE SHIT?

NIA. THAT'S A POSSIBILITY.

NOELLE. I'M SCARED OF GWEN.

NIA. GWEN'S A BEAST. SHE HAS FOUR KIDS.

NOELLE. HOW DOES THAT HAPPEN?

*(**NIA** looks at her.)*

DO YOU WANT KIDS? HOW CAN WE HANDLE KIDS? I CAN BARELY MAKE COFFEE –

---

*A license to produce *Project Dawn* does not include a performance license for any third-party or copyrighted music. Licensees should create an original composition or use music in the public domain. For further information, please see Music Use Note on page 3.

NIA. I COME HERE TO CHILL.

NOELLE. YEAH. YEAH NO SORRY. YEAH SURE.

(Lights out.)

BAILIFF'S VOICE. January court. We continue with the graduation speaker. Stay focused, stay focused. Limit your appreciation to the protocol of this court.

> *(**BONNIE** addresses the wildly enthusiastic group. She wears a newish outfit bought on a very limited budget. All but **GWEN** are the clients: **ASHLEE**, **KRYSTAL**, **TRACY**, **LOLA**, and **SHONDELL**. **SHONDELL** wears a patch over her eye.)*
>
> *(**BONNIE** is a practiced motivational speaker. She works the room with the drama, energy, and flair of a revival preacher. Even the painful parts of the story are crafted to warn her listeners.)*

BONNIE. This is a great day! Welcome families, friends, and representatives from City Hall here to witness success and get this court some money!

Who am I? You girls know me. I am Bonnie Mason. I am Shondell's sponsor. I am an activist. I am a lady in a relationship with a good and loving man! And I am a human being!

> *(Cheers from the group.)*

My whole life I've been Bonnie Mason but I wasn't sure on the rest a that list.

If it wasn't for Gwen McGowan and the Project Dawn Court I would be dead right now. Period. First time I met Gwen, I was coming through third floor and she was the public defender. Third floor you're a number, no one knows you. Next time I see Gwen it's two years later, I'm in jail, I caught a beating, I look different, but Gwen stares and says, "Bonnie is that you?" I was not remarkable I'll tell you that, just another junkie whore. But Gwen *knew me*: "Bonnie. Is that you?"

Gwen says I'm a perfect candidate for her new Project Dawn Court because I'm the worst of the worst. Fifty priors. But I never harmed no one but myself, is the story I told myself at the time. I wasn't looking at my sons. Or my big girl Lacy following Mom's ways.

I won't lie, I saw Project Dawn as a get out of jail free card. Any of you see it like that? But Gwen said some key words to me that kinda changed the scenery of that Monopoly board. Anyone remember those? Shondell?

SHONDELL. One. You must plead no contest to participate.

Two. You finish the program, they drop your charges.

Three. You don't comply, you get upstate for two point five to five, worse than if you never met Project Dawn in the first place. It's our choice. One two three.

BONNIE. Shondell I'm gonna see you up here in March!

I signed them no contest papers. Like all you here. Like Tamika, Courtney, and LeeAnn who finished all four phases and graduate today!

(Cheers from the group.)

Graduates, you are strong. That's what got you here. But respect the demon. Don't be so strong that you're weak.

I sign them papers for Gwen, and they send me to a twenty-eight-day rehab. How you gonna take an ex-prostitute, an addict, a sexual trauma survivor, and give her twenty-eight days and done? Twenty-eight days sober is just enough for the pain to rise.

I leave my rehab day twenty-nine. They tell me, "There's a bed at Our Heart to Your Heart, pack your things and head over. Do you need an escort?" I say no I'm good by myself. Right. The El passes right over Kensington Avenue and I think, I could be high *right now*. I could taste the numb. I step off the bus, and next thing I know it's three days later, seventeen degrees, I'm nodding out by the Pizza Hut trash can with frostbite, no underwear, a broken rib. A woman cop shakes me awake. She goes, "I'm arresting you," and I go, "No ma'am. You are saving me."

We all almost died. We *all* almost died.

Demons come shouting as soon as you're loose, especially when things don't go your way, and I will tell you a big secret: they mostly don't.

Gwen gave me a second chance. She helped me find a room at May's Place. I stood outside that big stone house and it looked like a doll house.

Just sitting down for dinner at May's Place with Sister Carol and them. I'm used to squatting on a corner eating a Little Debbie and a bag of chips trying not to miss the next trick. The first night I looked around the table and it reminded me of, it reminded me of the last supper.

I made a vow and a plan, and I kept that vow eight months with the support of Sister Carol and them. Then in the middle of the night Sister Carol knocks on my door, Bonnie you have a phone call. Hello? It's the police. Your daughter is dead.

My Lacy was twenty-one.

(She is feeling the pain, but also making sure the group feels it.)

I scream. I fall on the floor. I want to run. I want to get high. I want the pain to stop and I don't know how to make the pain stop except to *get* high. But this time I won't get high so I get very sick. I sit on my bed day after day. And Shondell Bridges *(Looks at* **SHONDELL**.*)* does not leave me alone.

SHONDELL. No I do not.

BONNIE. Every day she brought me something to eat.

SHONDELL. When you couldn't go down to the dining area, I'd tell you a dirty joke.

BONNIE. You asked about Lacy. I was not the mother I wanted to be.

SHONDELL. None of us was. I said you can die of guilt, or you can live with the guilt.

BONNIE. So that's what I do. Every day.

SHONDELL. You can't forgive yourself? Just get up.

BONNIE. You are my best friend and I love you.

SHONDELL. I love you too baby.

BONNIE. And my uncle used to say don't go with no black man. It wasn't the black ones beating me, raping me. I don't see color and that's the truth.

SHONDELL. That is nice for you baby.

BONNIE. Have respect for the demon. There's movie star millionaires can't kick this, you know what I'm saying? And they ain't sleeping at no Our Heart to Your Heart. But if you know you are smaller than your demon, you can change.

Judge Kaplan told me I had two minutes but I don't care because talking is my drug now. If I stub my toe I'm gonna tell you and if it still hurts I'm gonna tell you again.

Girls. I was a guest at Senator Dinniman's office last week helping him with the language for his anti-human trafficking bill. Bonnie Mason is helping to write a bill.

Now. I got fed a lot of stories as a child, but no one told me a story where I'm writing a *bill*, where I'm *changing* reality. And I like that story!

(*Applause.*)

I am with a man who *respects* me, who is *kind* to me, who if I don't feel like doing it, guess what?

SHONDELL. You don't do it!

(*Applause.*)

BONNIE. Girls, you will think about the life. You can let that thought become a feeling become an action. Or you can say:

"Uh-uh, Thought. I have plans, Thought. I'm gonna finish school, raise my kids, lean on others and become someone others lean upon."

Say it with me Shondell.

BONNIE & SHONDELL. God deals the deck, but we play the hand.

BONNIE. I love you graduates! I'm proud of you! Don't kill me Judge!

> *(The women give a rousing ovation, perhaps chanting, "Bonnie! Bonnie! Bonnie!")*
>
> *(End of the same day.* **NOELLE** *packs heavy boxes into the dolly. Gwen's paperwork still spread out.)*

GWEN. I need a replacement.

KYLA. I know you do.

GWEN. I'm dying here Kyla.

KYLA. This damn court was your idea.

GWEN. I have shitty shitty ideas.

KYLA. "Kyla, let's work the system to change the system. Kyla, you didn't become a DA to send girls to prison for hooking."

GWEN. No you became a DA because you want to sit on the Supreme Court.

KYLA. Third Circuit would be fine.

GWEN. All the glory, Kyla Grant. All the glory.

KYLA. Yeah I forgot I'm in this for the glory. Maybe if our girls can quit relapsing so we show some better numbers, Project Dawn Court will launch my mega career.

GWEN. How's your neck?

KYLA. Stiff. I requisitioned a new damn chair.

GWEN. Good luck with that.

KYLA. It'll loosen up after Taekwondo. You want to come? Free introductory session.

GWEN. HAH! I am training *all* the public defenders in the state. All those baby idealists. Four kids at home. And something else, whatsit…

NOELLE. Bryn Mawr.

GWEN. Right, I'm a professor at Bryn Mawr. I can't do this out of my back pocket anymore; it isn't fair to the girls.

KYLA. What's fair? Dumping them back to third floor: misdemeanor charge, girl too ashamed to come to court so her misdemeanor compounds: probation, failure to report, possession, prostitution, failure to report, bench warrant, failure to report? Prostitutes the most likely of all offenders to serve a maximum sentence. That's fair?

GWEN. You're right. You're right.

NOELLE. If it means anything at all, you're just so inspiring to so many people. You're my hero. Both of you.

KYLA. Shit.

GWEN. I'm not the hero. The clients are the heroes. I'm telling you, when the nukes hit, I'm following them.

KYLA. Me too.

GWEN. Our girls are like cockroaches. They survive.

NOELLE. Do you think it's their choice?

GWEN & KYLA. *Choice?*

NOELLE. I have friends who dance for tuition and – as a feminist I believe women should control our bodies. I've been reading –

KYLA. You want to give blowjobs on the Ave or you want to be in court with Gwen?

NOELLE. Court. But do you believe in a continuum? Like, from what happened to Ashlee to –

GWEN. The "sex-positive sex workers"?

NOELLE. Yeah.

GWEN. I suppose they exist, because they heckle me when I speak about ending modern slavery, but they don't come through my court.

NOELLE. Why not?

GWEN. Our girls are easy to find. Low-hanging fruit.

KYLA. And remember they have to confess up front. Maybe the online entrepreneurs think they can beat the ticket.

NOELLE. So the indoor girls are different.

GWEN. Every prostitute woman I ever met, from every social class, was sexually abused as a child. One hundred percent. She'll say, "I don't have a pimp." I tell you what, her first pimp was the abuser. He helped himself to a product, a human being, and now she thinks she's going to get wise and sell the product. It's power but it's false power.

KYLA. Those "sex workers" claiming "it's a career choice," first of all many of them are madams protecting business interests. Secondly these people tend to be left-wing liberals, but they go marketplace libertarian in this *one arena*. Why?

GWEN. How do you feel about sale of organs?

NOELLE. Organs?

GWEN. Shouldn't poor people get to make a choice, sell off a kidney? A lung? A chunk of liver?

NOELLE. No!

KYLA. Flesh trade. Same thing. One hooker with a book deal won't change the equation.

NOELLE. But –

GWEN. Furthermore, if it's a career choice how come they can't do it sober? Do your friends dance sober?

NOELLE. Actually no.

GWEN. I might need to drink a bottle of wine *after* work but I don't need to drink a bottle of wine to go *to* work. That's the difference!

NOELLE. Wow.

KYLA. A bottle, Gwen?

GWEN. You don't remember; a bottle's small.

KYLA. Oh I remember.

*(**NIA** on her way out.)*

GWEN. Nia, nothing on Cassie?

NIA. She got her surgery in December, she took the painkiller and she walked out. AWOL.

KYLA. Can we check Sister Carol's drop-in center?

GWEN. Sister Carol's service is anonymous.

KYLA. I need to know if Cassie is on the Ave. Can we get Sister Carol into court?

GWEN. You want to force an eighty-year-old activist nun to testify against her women?

NIA. I'd rather subpoena Jesus.

KYLA. Can we *invite* Sister Carol to court?

NIA. I'll ask the judge.

*(She exits. **RUTH** on her way out.)*

KYLA. You look nice Ruth.

RUTH. Anniversary dinner. The children are treating us.

KYLA. You enjoy yourself.

RUTH. We always do.

(She exits.)

NOELLE. I still don't understand why we don't try the men.

KYLA. Because this is prostitution court not Johns Court.

NOELLE. They should fund the Johns Court.

GWEN. They should fund *this* fucking court.

KYLA. Also Gwen should return a favor once in a while and start the Johns Court with her buddy Kyla. Get the bad guys. *That's* why I'm a DA.

GWEN. Except Gwen is going to physically die if she gets one more responsibility. Plus after twenty years in the field, if Gwen ever entered a room of motherfucking johns she might commit serial homicide, giving Kyla one more criminal to prosecute.

KYLA. *(To **NOELLE**, for **GWEN**'s benefit.)* How come each girl's got ten twenty johns a night and the cops pick up thirty girls a *day* and thirty men maybe once a *year*?

NOELLE. That's disgusting! That's so unfair!

GWEN. Don't get me started Noelle, I'm serious I have high cholesterol.

(She eats a Little Debbie snack cake. As explanation:)

Lunch.

NOELLE. Is that a Little Debbie snack cake?

KYLA. Jesus Christ Gwen, bring a salad.

GWEN. I DON'T WANT A DAMN SALAD, I'M STRESSED. Stop trying to micromanage everybody. I don't have a wife. I walk in my door eight p.m. the damn chicken is still frozen!

KYLA. My wife would make you a salad.

GWEN. I should have been a nun.

KYLA. I'm booking you a massage and paying in advance. Don't waste my money.

> (**GWEN** *checks her phone and sees a string of texts.*)

GWEN. Shit.

NOELLE. Where do you need me, boss?

GWEN. Meredith was supposed to pick up Joey, she left her bus pass at home, and Joey's stranded. Shit shit shit. I put the bus pass on the table with a Post-it. I put another Post-it on the door. I sent her a text saying read the Post-its. Shit shit shit what is *wrong* with people?

> (*She exits.* **NOELLE** *finishes packing the boxes.*)

KYLA. You okay with those?

NOELLE. I'm great. Have a good night.

KYLA. You too, Nicole.

> (*She leaves.*)

NOELLE. (*My name is.*) Noelle?

> (*She loads the boxes onto her dolly. She struggles with the weight. One spills but she catches it in some painful way. With all her strength, she puts the box right.*)
>
> (*Light shift.*)
>
> (**GWEN** *yells at her kids. A glass of wine handy though she is lucid. The words "blessed," "the birds," etc. sound like the filthiest curses.*)

GWEN. No I am not paying you back the four fifty. Because I didn't leave your bus pass at home. *You* left your bus pass at home.

Meredith Joanne how is your bus pass my responsibility?

Uh-huh.

Uh-huh.

So by that logic every *blessed* thing in this house is my responsibility because by pitching in to the household that feeds, clothes, and supports us all, you are only always and perpetually covering for *me*? Is that the logic? Every *blessed* thing that gets done around here gets done for *Mom*? For *Gwen*? You better study harder if you want to be a lawyer because your logic is for *the birds*.

Let's start with your premise that picking up Joey was my responsibility – Joey you are part of this conversation too, *everybody* is part of this conversation even Dad who's out – *get in here Joey*.

Everyone is part of this *blessed* conversation.

Everyone is part of this *blessed* home.

I am an intelligent individual, I'm told between eight a.m. and six or seven or nine p.m. Monday through Friday sometimes Saturday and occasionally Sunday evening. Hundreds of college graduates apply every year to work for me, for minimum wage which I pay out of my pocket. Most would do it for free but I don't take free interns because you know *why*? Because I cannot spend my *blessed* work days with entitled children and do you know *why*? Meredith Joanne? Joseph Andrew? Frances Connor? James Michael? Can any of you explain to me why I refuse to hire college graduates who can afford to work for free meaning ipso facto that Mom and Dad are underwriting their "careers"?

Because when someone works for you for free *you* owe *them*. They swap labor for experience and mentorship and whatever the *flip* else. I can't swap. I need to walk into my office, regard a young person blooming up at me, and say, get the cartons in the hand truck.

And when I look up again I need to see the cartons in the hand truck.

And the next time there's a pile of boxes I need them in the hand truck before I ask.

I can't owe anyone another *blessed* thing. I would argue I *don't* owe anyone another blessed thing. It is time it is time it is time for us to become a little more of a unit, people. A little more of some step up, people.

(*Meredith talks.* **GWEN** *unloads scorn.*)

Obviously you didn't birth your brother. That is the lamest excuse, come on Merry our brains work to a higher standard. *Obviously* you didn't choose to be the eldest. But what's the statute of limitations? I went to school in Uncle Pete's shoes, am I calling Granny now to ask for a new pair? *You eat the four fifty.*

(*Withering.*) You can too breathe. You're breathing right now or you wouldn't whine.

A little more participation, all of you! A little more democracy in action!

(*A doorbell we don't hear.*)

Pizza's here. Wash our hands and say grace.

BAILIFF'S VOICE. February court.

Numbers thirty-five, twenty-six, and eighty-seven. Miss Ashlee Fuller.

(**ASHLEE** *stands in front of the court, weeping.* **GWEN** *is kind.* **RUTH** *and* **NIA** *as staff;* **SHONDELL** *and* **TRACY** *as clients.*)

GWEN. Your Honor, this is Miss Ashlee Fuller. The court has had some problems locating her, she resides with her grandmother, but the grandmother had no contact. Ashlee hasn't reported to group, to me. Radio silence. We're worried.

JUDGE. Hello Ashlee.

(**ASHLEE** *bawls.*)

Reviewing your test results, we are all trying to find the missing piece. I'm seeing a positive for Benzos higher than prescribed but then you have another urine with zero Benzos. Your prescribed meds should show up on the test. So either you're sharing or you are dosing yourself in some bizarre way. Can you help us out here Ashlee?

(**ASHLEE** *bawls.*)

GWEN. Oh honey.

JUDGE. Ruth have you had a chance to meet with Ashlee?

RUTH. No Your Honor. She missed her sessions.

JUDGE. Okay Ashlee, we're going to come back to you at the end of court.

(**ASHLEE** *bawls.*)

We want to make sure you have an opportunity to get some support from Ruth.

GWEN. You can sit down sweetheart.

ASHLEE. Thank you.

(**SHONDELL** *grunts in protest.*)

SHONDELL. I'm a sweetheart too.

TRACY. If you have a complaint make your damn complaint but don't call her racist.

SHONDELL. Who said racist.

TRACY. Ashlee is a baby.

SHONDELL. We all was babies.

TRACY. She got kidnapped. Cuffed to a hook in a van. Had to trick with how many men a night, almost a year.

SHONDELL. Average age of entry into the street is thirteen, some young as six or seven.

TRACY. Sober the whole time, remembers the whole thing. He had no pity even to buy her drugs.

SHONDELL. They should be trying us as children because you do not progress. In your emotional you do not progress. I was a princess. I wore a new dress every day.

TRACY. That's the past. The motherfucking future is in our hands. God deals the deck but we play the hand, right?

SHONDELL. Deck be stacked *and* rules be breaking.

(JUDGE's gavel.)

BAILIFF'S VOICE. No talking. No selfies. No gum.

Numbers twenty-seven, twenty-eight, thirty-one, and sixty-four. Krystal Williams.

(GWEN stands with KRYSTAL, who wears a hijab but not the veil.)

GWEN. Your Honor, this is Ms. Krystal Williams. She is still living with her uncle and attends IOP at Step Ahead.

JUDGE. Hello Krystal. How is it at your uncle's?

KRYSTAL. It's okay; building inspector come around but my uncle says don't worry.

NIA. Skyline Homes has nine outstanding violations.

JUDGE. Is that an immediate threat to Krystal's housing?

NIA. Not in Philly.

GWEN. Your Honor, Krystal would like to tell you something good.

JUDGE. I am ready to hear it.

KRYSTAL. They invited me to tell my story to some younger girls at Step Ahead!

JUDGE. That's a real honor.

KRYSTAL. I was sweating so hard I had to change clothes three times. I about went through all the long sleeves in Nia's shopping closet.

JUDGE. How did it go?

KRYSTAL. Your Honor, I used Ruth's framework! I told what happened to me, how it affects me now, what I need to heal. I told about my power spark.

Some of those girls started crying. They're so young. When I was that young I didn't know I was that young, you know?

JUDGE. I'm very proud of you, Krystal.

KRYSTAL. You never said that before.

JUDGE. Well it's the truth. Anything to add, Ms. Grant?

KYLA. Very nice work, Krystal. We're all rooting for you.

KRYSTAL. *(To* **KYLA.***)* We shall overcome!

KYLA. See you in March. That will be phase four.

KRYSTAL. YES.

> *(Delighted, she sits down.* **SISTER CAROL** *enters with a walker.)*

JUDGE. Sister Carol, welcome.

SISTER CAROL. I have urgent work this morning, but I am *invited* to serve the court. I'll be seated.

> *(She sits.)*

Please proceed.

JUDGE. Thank you.

BAILIFF'S VOICE. Violations number sixty-seven and seventy-three, Miss Lola Vargas.

> *(***LOLA*** stands [shifting from* **NIA***].)*

GWEN. Your Honor this is Ms. Lola Vargas. In December Lola requested permission to travel to see her estranged mother in California.

LOLA. My mom wants to buy it before the prices go up.

JUDGE. I understand. Have you met with the nutritionist?

LOLA. Not yet, Your Honor.

JUDGE. Well, meet with her and then we'll talk about your ticket.

LOLA. *(Timid.)* Your Honor? You're asking me every month did I eat a cookie, know what I mean?

JUDGE. I'm not sure I do.

LOLA. *(Timid.)* Where are the Mummers?

JUDGE. Pardon?

LOLA. Never mind.

NOELLE. *(To* **GWEN.***)* What are Mummers?

GWEN. Mummers Party Prostitution Raid. Google it.

JUDGE. The owners who *ran* the party were indicted.

KYLA. There were eighty men the night of the raid, and those parties were regular events.

NOELLE. *(Reading from her phone.)* Holy shit.

LOLA. Ms. Grant I appreciate your presence. It's like having a man in here.

KYLA. I'm glad that's working out for you, Ms. Vargas.

LOLA. Is it true you have a wife?

KYLA. Yes that's true.

LOLA. Good for you. We've all done everything with everybody so I'm not going to say anything is disgusting. I fucked a horse. I fucked three men together at that Mummers party.

I was wrong. I was a whore. But I lost everything. I lost my little girl to the system. I just wonder, what happened to the men?

KYLA. It's a valid question.

*(***SISTER CAROL** *speaks in a holy rage:)*

SISTER CAROL. I'll tell you what happened to the men! They grew up in a culture that says **we need prostitutes for men**.

JUDGE. Sister Carol. We appreciate your time.

*(***SISTER CAROL** *stands.)*

SISTER CAROL. Your Honor, if I inform on the women, they won't attend the drop-in center and they will forgo the small necessities we provide.

JUDGE. We are worried about Cassie, and believe you might have seen her.

SISTER CAROL. Do you want the information in order to help Cassie, or to prosecute her?

JUDGE. Support and accountability are related.

SISTER CAROL. You hold the power to subpoena me and force my testimony.

JUDGE. I don't want to do that.

SISTER CAROL. These women are *victims* of a culture that says it's okay to use prostitutes. Songs, jokes, entertainment all say you can buy a person for sex, go ahead. No one is going to take that liberty from the man, the man must have the liberty to rob another of her liberty and humanity and dignity.

There are more slaves in the world now than at any point in history.

JUDGE. We share your concern, / Sister Carol. All of us are –

SISTER CAROL. More than twenty million human souls are in bondage today. That is more than during what we think of as slave times. The Rohingya people have been expelled from Thailand, they are bought and sold – the boats that stored fish now store people. Some are sold for sex and some are sold for their labor.

JUDGE. Under the law, we distinguish between trafficked persons / and prostitution.

SISTER CAROL. Power over the weak enforced by brutality.
And we do not care. Our culture does not care.
Where is the rage?

JUDGE. It is a process, Sister Carol.

SISTER CAROL. I'm on this side of the fence, I don't need to follow the process. We held some lovely anti-trafficking meetings in Philadelphia, "awareness raising activities," but where is the underlying what I would call rage to say **this has to stop**?

I served thirty years as a nurse midwife in so-called developing countries, war-torn societies: Beirut, Rwanda, Sierra Leone. When I returned to Philadelphia for what I thought was a retirement ministry, I found that the condition of our women here, physically, psychologically, even nutritionally is equal to what I saw there.

It is challenging and heartbreaking and makes you so angry at an affluent society that we have women and children on the streets.

I founded May's Place. But May's Place must have rules, and some souls are not ready for rules. They may never change. Yet they too deserve love and help. So I founded my drop-in center for women who are still on the street and need a respite, no questions asked. Comfort and dignity for a night, for an hour, in a world in which they are lost. And today you ask me to betray even that small privacy.

When I sit and break bread with women who are the outcasts of society, or when I comb a lady's hair after she has bathed, that is my glance into the Kingdom of God. That's what it will be like in heaven. We will sit with our brothers and sisters and it won't matter what they've done or where they've been.

I have no interest in prosecuting women and unless you force me to do so I will not assist.

KYLA. Sister Carol with all respect, do you want Cassie to die?

SISTER CAROL. I am not a judge. I will not bring a victim to judgment.

KYLA. You give women baths so they can OD on the street? That makes no sense. The clients need consequences, order, accountability.

SISTER CAROL. Project Dawn Court is a fine program and you respect the women's humanity and you do it without exploding into rage, which I don't believe I could do.

I have served God for eighty years across this earth and still I fear I will die angry.

*(She turns and leaves the court. **KYLA** can leave with her.)*

JUDGE. Lola.

LOLA. Your Honor?

JUDGE. Tell your mother to buy the ticket.

*(**LOLA** raises her arms in victory.)*

LOLA. Thank you, Your Honor.

JUDGE. Please bring us a detailed report from California, and some good weather.

LOLA. I'ma eat oranges out there, Your Honor. Very healthy!

JUDGE. Next client.

*(In the women's bathroom, **NOELLE** discovers **SHONDELL** on the toilet with the stall door open. She yelps loudly.)*

NOELLE. Excuse me!

SHONDELL. You never saw a lady on a toilet?

NOELLE. My people shut the door.

SHONDELL. Are you a Quaker?

NOELLE. Lutheran.

SHONDELL. Are you a virgin?

NOELLE. What are you talking about?

SHONDELL. I'd feel bad for you in with us, a virgin.

NOELLE. I have sex! Damn! I mean that's not really my job, to discuss personal matters with clients.

SHONDELL. Naw that sharing only flows one way.

(NIA walks in. Unfazed by the toilet scene.)

NIA. Court's in session, Shondell.

SHONDELL. Stall door is broke.

NIA. Worked okay for me. Get back in there.

(She walks out. KRYSTAL walks in.)

KRYSTAL. Ooh, there a line?

SHONDELL. Hannah Montana needs to go.

NOELLE. I'm okay.

KRYSTAL. Good.

(She enters a stall.)

NOELLE. Close the door please.

(KRYSTAL pees behind the stall door.)

KRYSTAL. Ahh.

NOELLE. *(Vaguely making an exit.)* I'll see you all in there.

SHONDELL. *(To NOELLE.)* Hold up sweetie will you check my eye.

(Straight from the stall, she reaches to take off her eyepatch.)

NOELLE. You should wash your hands for twenty seconds.

SHONDELL. Go on.

(TRACY enters. It's now pretty crowded.)

TRACY. Whoa. We oughta get hall passes. Remember them?

NOELLE. Yeah, sure.

KRYSTAL. *(From stall.)* Hall pass. You're funny.

SHONDELL. I didn't go to no public school. I was a princess.

TRACY. I forgot. Crack royalty.

SHONDELL. I ain't jumping on no bait. Lucky for you, I unhooked from that bait.

> *(**TRACY** lights a cigarette.)*

NOELLE. Are you supposed to smoke?

KRYSTAL. *(In stall.)* Would you get me some paper Honey Boo Boo?

NOELLE. *(Decides she can be called Honey Boo Boo.)* No problem.

KRYSTAL. Thanks baby.

> *(**NOELLE** hands her toilet paper, then washes her hands vigorously.)*

SHONDELL. I need to know, is it better or worse?

> *(**NOELLE** takes off **SHONDELL**'s eyepatch. We don't see, but it's horrible. **NOELLE** jumps back from the sink, splashing a huge amount of water on herself. It looks like she peed. **TRACY** and **SHONDELL** crack up.)*

TRACY. Whoa girl hold your water.

NOELLE. It's from the sink.

SHONDELL. Just a little scar scare the piss out of you?

NOELLE. You saw it's the sink.

> *(She tries to get paper towels.)*

TRACY. Machine's broke.

KRYSTAL. *(From stall.)* Toddler Tiara go pee pee?

NOELLE. STOP BEING JUVENILE.

> *(She grabs a bunch of toilet paper from the empty stall. She blots the outside of her pants with the toilet paper.)*

TRACY. That is not gonna work.

(She is subtly blocking the entrance to the stall.)

NOELLE. Fuck it.

(She takes off her pants, pulls a pair of short leggings out of her bag, and changes.)

TRACY. Those are some foxy panties, girl.

SHONDELL. Not a virgin with those underwears.

NOELLE. Oh my god.

TRACY. Don't stress. You look good.

NOELLE. Thanks.

SHONDELL. You got a nice butt for a white girl.

NOELLE. Thank you.

TRACY. You want some ink on that ass? Make you unforgettable.

NOELLE. No thank you Tracy, but I wish you the best with your business.

(Her change is successful, and her outfit looks okay.)

TRACY. You just carry pants in your bag?

NOELLE. It's *spin night*.

(She exits with all the attitude she can muster. **KRYSTAL, TRACY,** *and* **SHONDELL** *laugh hard.)*

SHONDELL. Spin Night.

TRACY. Spin what?

(The women spin in some way, escalating into a dance. **SHONDELL**'s *eye suddenly hurts her.)*

You need me to clean out that eye for you? I got my no-sting antiseptic with me.

SHONDELL. Thank you baby.

TRACY. You should let me do some art near your scar. On the house.

SHONDELL. That's a nice offer baby, but no one's touching my wound.

(*Back to the courtroom. Late the same day.*)

JUDGE. And that brings us back to Ashlee.

(**ASHLEE** *enters, still badly shaken.*)

GWEN. Your Honor, this is Ms. Ashlee –

(**ASHLEE** *bawls.*)

Ruth and Ashlee had a session in the side room. Ruth?

RUTH. The pain is there without a framework.

(**ASHLEE** *bawls.*)

The therapeutic process assumes a modality of hope. And Ashlee is in despair.

ASHLEE. I just keep seeing this one guy's face. I'm not tricking. I can't have sex with no one, I'm so ashamed of myself.

JUDGE. All we want you to do when you feel like you're getting into trouble, is ask for help. You have Gwen, and Ruth, and Nia –

ASHLEE. Nia hates me.

NIA. (*From work phone.*) Not true.

ASHLEE. You called me a liar.

NIA. You give me bad numbers. I can't find you. I want to find you.

JUDGE. We are afraid for your life.

ASHLEE. I'm nothing. I'm a whore.

RUTH. We see you as precious and worth protecting.

(**ASHLEE** *bawls.*)

JUDGE. With the poison heroin going around on the street, we are all afraid you're going to get a bad bag and die.

ASHLEE. Not my luck.

(*Beat.*)

KYLA. See you say things like that and we get scared.

JUDGE. We are down to very few options. Even if I could jump you over everyone else to get you into an inpatient program, Nia tells me no one will take you with the Suboxone in your system.

NIA. *(Still on phone.)* Gibson will do methadone; no one will take the Suboxone.

ASHLEE. I went to hell.

RUTH. You survived.

ASHLEE. I did not.

RUTH. Somewhere inside, you did.

KYLA. You use the Suboxone to supplement heroin.

(**ASHLEE** *starts to panic.*)

ASHLEE. I only take the Suboxone because it's a blocker, so as I *won't* take heroin.

KYLA. You can't pick and choose, Ashlee. The drug regimen is not your decision. You are not a doctor.

ASHLEE. Neither are you.

KYLA. I'm going to let that go.

ASHLEE. Your Honor, have faith in me.

JUDGE. If I have to weigh having faith in you and knowing you'll be alive –

ASHLEE. I'll go to my grandma's. That's a stable place for me.

NIA. We've been calling Grandma and you don't stay there. You go to Mom's. And Mom is not a good influence.

KYLA. Is Mom taking your Suboxone hon?

ASHLEE. *Please don't embarrass me!*

GWEN. Your Honor, for the record this is a real Catch-22 where they won't take her inpatient unless she's clean, but she has no structured housing in which to get clean on her own. Ashlee's choices are so severely limited.

KYLA. I recommend ninety days in county.

(**ASHLEE** *wails.*)

GWEN. I remind the court that Ashlee was a minor when a man approached her on the street, offering heroin.

ASHLEE. Chained me to a wall in the day. Gave me heels didn't even fit. Made me walk around a White Castle at night. I don't even know where in DC I was. Just near a White Castle.

GWEN. For ten months.

ASHLEE. He said he'd give me drugs but I never saw no drugs. I didn't kidnap no one and chain them up and make them trick all night *sober*.

JUDGE. Ashlee. You were a victim. In my worst nightmare I can't imagine. The man in question did time.

KYLA. He's out.

ASHLEE. I'm gonna be sick.

JUDGE. But now you are an adult. You caught your own cases.

KYLA. Fifteen of them.

JUDGE. You are skipping therapy.

ASHLEE. I thought that was private.

RUTH. You know your attendance record is not private, Ashlee.

ASHLEE. It's not my fault.

> (**NIA** *takes a message on paper, walks the paper over to* **GWEN**. **GWEN** *reads it and sits down.*)

JUDGE. Ashlee. I'm going to let you go one more month.

ASHLEE. Thank you!

KYLA. May I call a sidebar, Your Honor?

> (*Sidebar light.* **KYLA** *fuming.* **GWEN** *stays seated, focused on the note from Nia.*)

Your Honor, I respectfully suggest the court is emotionally influenced by Ashlee. She is young. She is white. She has been MIA this entire month. She cannot remain in the program. I'm defending my time on this court up the chain of command. Three years in, our recidivism rates are too high.

JUDGE. Counsel? Gwen?

GWEN. What?

JUDGE. Step up to sidebar please.

> (**GWEN** *does.*)

KYLA. We must be aware of cultural bias, or we perpetuate a system in which a white girl's innocence is more powerful than a black girl's innocence. The other participants are watching. Ashlee used. She must be accountable.

JUDGE. Kyla, you are suggesting that Ashlee received preferential treatment because of race?

KYLA. Not consciously.

JUDGE. You are not suggesting it consciously?

KYLA. You made an exception for Cassie, Your Honor, because she was in pain. All our clients are in pain. If they can't be held accountable, what are we doing in court? We must be consistent with the hug and the hammer.

JUDGE. Ruth? Hug or hammer?

RUTH. Your Honor...this is a larger question. I recently attended a retreat on Power in the Workplace. I could lead a staff session that might –

JUDGE. Yes. Good. Before court next month. Gwen?

GWEN. Sorry I didn't follow.

KYLA. You didn't *follow*?

NIA. Meredith is missing.

> (*Beat.*)

RUTH. Your daughter Meredith?

> (**GWEN** *nods.*)

KYLA. How long?

NIA. Two days.

RUTH. Gwen I didn't know.

GWEN. I didn't know either.

> (*She exits.* **KYLA** *follows her.*)
>
> (**JUDGE** *raps with gavel. Lights back to normal.*)

JUDGE. Ashlee. Sixty days.
ASHLEE. NOOOO...
TRACY. Come on. I took shits longer than that.

> *(Night.* **GWEN** *wanders Kensington Avenue, epicenter of street prostitution and heroin trafficking, looking for her daughter. It feels like a nightmare but it's real.)*

GWEN. Meredith? Merrie? *Meredith?*

> *(***KYLA*** appears, maybe from a different direction.)*

KYLA. Gwen what the hell? I've been looking for you everywhere.

GWEN. MEREDITH?

KYLA. Your daughter is not on the Ave.

GWEN. It happened to Ashlee. It happened to Meredith. MERRIE?

KYLA. Honey, Ashlee was an addict. Her mother is an addict. Meredith has you and Joe.

GWEN. MEREDITH QUIT HIDING QUIT FAKING!

KYLA. We gotta get you home. It's scary here.

GWEN. I know this place.

KYLA. The Ave?

GWEN. I was a kid near here.

KYLA. You got out. You don't have to go back. Your daughter is never gonna see this place. Okay?

GWEN. MEREDITH?

KYLA. Let's think about where she might actually be. Does she have a car?

GWEN. HAH.

KYLA. Who does she love?

GWEN. I don't know her at all.

> *(She almost trips on a figure hidden under a blanket.)*

Merrie? Ashlee? Cassie?

PERSON UNDER BLANKET. Thirty to suck, sixty to fuck.

KYLA. Miss can we help you find a shelter? It's gonna freeze tonight.

>   (**GWEN** *crouches down. She recognizes* **BONNIE**.)

GWEN. *(Gently.)* Bonnie? Is that you?

BONNIE. Gwen knew me.

>   (**GWEN** *explodes.*)

GWEN. FUCK YOU.

>   (*She punches* **BONNIE**. **KYLA** *restrains her in a Taekwondo move.*)

KYLA. No, Gwen.

GWEN. Six years of my life. FUCK YOU. Visiting up Muncy. Shoulda spent weekends with my own kids. FUCK YOU.

KYLA. Let's go, Gwen.

BONNIE. My man left me.

GWEN. WHAT A WASTE!

KYLA. Up and out.

>   (*She gets* **GWEN** *up.*)

BONNIE. No home. No girl.

GWEN. 'Cause you're a *junkie*.

KYLA. Don't punk out on us, Gwen. We need you.

>   (*As she walks* **GWEN** *out,* **GWEN** *loses her anger, looks back:*)

GWEN. Bonnie. Is that you?

KYLA. I'm getting *you* home.

>   (*She and* **GWEN** *leave* **BONNIE**. **BONNIE** *sees a clear vision of her daughter.*)

BONNIE. Hi, Lacy!

>   (*She reaches for Lacy. Her speech is lucid.*)

My beautiful baby. I missed you.

ACT TWO

(While intermission house lights are still up, **RUTH** *sets up an early morning therapy session for the staff.)*

(If the **BAILIFF** *is played live, she is part of the workshop and shows up first.* **RUTH** *seats her.)*

*(***NIA*** enters.* **RUTH** *seats each person at a spot that is not their usual place. The* **JUDGE** *wanders into the main part of the court wearing regular clothes in a soft color.)*

NIA. Good morning, Your Honor.

JUDGE. Good morning, Nia.

RUTH. There might be a few more participants.

JUDGE. I can go and come back.

RUTH. Please stay Your Honor. It's ten after. We can start.

NIA. Are we going to be sharing our emotions out loud?

RUTH. I'll explain the structure.

(She looks to see if someone else is coming. No. She commits fully. She is good at this. She passes out legal pads.)

(Her presentation includes the audience as much as possible without leaving the reality of the courtroom. Please see more thoughts on Ruth's writing workshop at the end of the script.)

This workshop, A User's Guide to Power, is designed to support counselors, activists, and criminal justice workers in a personal process of analyzing power. Our assumptions about power impact our own mental health, as well as our understanding of justice and responsibility. Thank you for attending.

(KYLA shows up in the doorway.)

RUTH. Kyla! Please take a seat. We are just getting started. I am glad you are here.

KYLA. My pleasure. Are we reading out loud?

RUTH. That seems to be the question of the day. We will primarily be writing, with the option to reflect. Everyone has something to write with?

(KYLA uses an iPad.)

No Gwen?

NIA. She's been very slow with e-mail and her phone is off. She should at least be here in time for court.

RUTH. All right.

About one third to one half of therapeutic and criminal justice professionals are trauma survivors. That's double the general population percentage. In other words, we are working through our own Ish. Thank you Judge Kaplan for responding to my suggestion that we begin this deep work for ourselves.

JUDGE. You're welcome.

RUTH. I like to give credit where credit is due, for a change, in this case my mentor Vanessa Jackson of Atlanta, Georgia who designed these questions and wrote *Power: A User's Manual*.

We begin. I will read the questions and you write your answers.

What is your working definition of power?

NIA. Pardon?

RUTH. What's your personal definition of power.

NIA. Okay.

*(The women write. If the **BAILIFF** is onstage, she tends to start first and finish first. Perhaps the audience writes too. Let this take a while.)*

RUTH. How does this definition of power shape your experience of being powerful or powerless?

KYLA. Which one?

RUTH. Either. Or both. How does this definition of power shape your experience of being powerful or powerless?

> *(The women write.)*

JUDGE. This is very interesting, Ruth.

RUTH. I'm glad, Your Honor.
Think back to an early time when you felt powerful.

> *(KYLA and the JUDGE start writing immediately. NIA thinks.)*

What was the context? Who was present? What was the nature of the interaction?

> *(NIA identifies the moment and writes.)*

How, if at all, does this event influence your life today?

> *(All the women write with gusto. See what happens if this goes on for a couple minutes.)*

Good. Good. You want to hang onto this. This is your Power Spark. A durable memory of yourself as a powerful being. This is very important.
Now. Think back to a time when you felt powerless.

> *(The women look blankly at RUTH.)*

KYLA. We aren't reading out loud?

> *(NIA starts to write.)*

RUTH. This can stay private.
Think back to a time when you felt powerless.
What was the context?
Who was present?

> *(KYLA writes.)*

What was the nature of the interaction?

> *(KYLA and NIA write. The JUDGE looks at her paper. She bends over her paper and starts to write.)*

How, if at all, does this event influence your life today?

> *(All three women write. It goes on for a while.)*

RUTH. Okay, finish up whatever sentence you are on.

> (**KYLA** and **NIA** stop writing, the **JUDGE** still buried in her paper.)
>
> (**KYLA** and **NIA** look at **RUTH**. The **JUDGE** is still absorbed in writing. Awkward.)

Any new understandings about power and how it operates in your life?

> (Beat.)

Let's acknowledge the power differential among us on staff. Economics are a factor, race is a factor, education and professional status are factors. Let's honor all of that.

What insights came up as you answered the questions?

> (The **JUDGE** sobs. She covers her mouth.)

JUDGE. Thank you, Ruth. Excuse me.

> (She exits to her chambers. Awkward.)

NIA. Really great workshop, Ruth. Nice job.

RUTH. I could use a dozen donuts.

KYLA. On me.

RUTH. You don't eat the trans fats.

KYLA. You made the judge cry. It's an emergency.

RUTH. Holy Ish.

NIA. You know what?

RUTH. What, Nia?

NIA. I got nothing. Let's eat donuts.

RUTH. You go on. Bring me back something bad. I'm going to check on the judge.

NIA. You are?

RUTH. I'm trained.

> (**KYLA** and **NIA** exit. **RUTH** pursues the **JUDGE**. Lights out. **BAILIFF**'s voice in darkness:)

BAILIFF'S VOICE. March court is now in session. Honorable Judge Roberta Kaplan presiding. No texting. No selfies. No gum.

(*The* **JUDGE** *back on the bench.* **NOELLE, NIA,** *and* **RUTH** *as staff.* **SHONDELL** *and* **TRACY** *as clients. Everyone notices* **GWEN** *is missing. The* **JUDGE** *vamps.*)

JUDGE. We have a graduate this morning. Let's start there. Ruth?

RUTH. Your Honor, this is Ms. Shondell Bridges. Ms. Bridges is a graduate of May's Place. She is now living with her son and granddaughters; she works in housekeeping at the Comfort Suites. She is completing phase four and graduates today.

(*Cheers from the women, especially* **TRACY**.)

JUDGE. Wonderful, Shondell. Do you have any words to offer to the women who aspire to be in your shoes one day?

SHONDELL. I didn't learn shit from my experience.

JUDGE. We are proud of you anyway.

SHONDELL. This ain't my graduation without Bonnie. She's my sponsor. I'm worried for her. And where's Gwen?

JUDGE. Are you saying you'd prefer to get more subpoenas and owe us more time?

SHONDELL. Hell no. I just didn't picture this by myself.

RUTH. It's been a tough month.

SHONDELL. I thought my eye was gonna heal by now and look right. It don't hurt much. I can see shapes. But I feel branded. Maybe I'm just depressed.

RUTH. Shondell, if we're going to talk about your depression –

SHONDELL. We need to talk about my oppression. I been listening, Ruth.

RUTH. I know you have.

SHONDELL. It's a happy moment but I'm not feeling it.

RUTH. Is there anything you're looking forward to, Shondell?

SHONDELL. Grandma things.

RUTH. What are grandma things?

SHONDELL. I like to bake. I want my grandbabies to have those memories of me, Grandma who bakes the lemon bars.

RUTH. That's a good start.

SHONDELL. I suppose I do have some words.

JUDGE. Please.

SHONDELL. I was a princess. I never played outside with nobody. Everyone came to me. Everyone bought me presents. I didn't have no problem with drugs, I had all the drugs I wanted. I was popular 'cause I could give out the free drugs, my uncle never said no to me. Everything I wanted, I got, from little girl things through big girl things. It was a blessed childhood.

I never worked anywhere; my uncle said that was slavery. He paid my fees to Temple, I flunked out. He paid for beauty school which I didn't flunk – obviously – but I never wanted to touch someone else's head.

I was spoiled. Then I was busy with my son. Then my uncle died and I had my demand without my supply. And I had some so-called friends, we started out just partying a little you know, you have something I want, I have something you want, and to be honest with you I didn't mind. Best times of my life were young and high. There is no feeling on this earth beats young and high. Speaking from old and sober, I'm telling you facts.

(Her eye.) My attack happened just last year. What's a grandma doing fighting off a bad trick trying to carve up my face?

I see the life. I see it at the Comfort Suites. I don't feel too bad for them mostly, they are indoors. A hot shower after, me to clean the sheets.

The boys are the worst. I don't know if they're all hustling or if that's just how they play. You can't pay me enough to clean those rooms, but I guess you can because I do it. And they tip. Jesus lord they make a gruesome mess but they tip.

At May's Place we had some foreign girls. Three beautiful girls from Indonesia I believe. They spoke no English, they didn't know where they were, no phones, no maps. These pimps from their own country were pulling them city to city every couple days.

No one forced me, coerced me, tricked me which is the legal definition of trafficking. But Ruth helped me to identify some of the factors that led to my vulnerability, when my uncle died. Like, why was I raised in illegal wealth rather than legal wealth? How in the white culture the illegal wealth might lead to legal wealth for future generations, like the mafia, or killing Indians, or the steel men? Whereas in the black culture the illegal wealth leads to butts locked up, one generation after the next. We never hold our ill-got gains.

That's a structure. It ain't an excuse but it's a structure.

Now I make my way by daylight. By my light. I have a friend. He is sometimes a friend with benefits but that is a different matter. A very different matter.

Men are not changing their ways any time soon.

There's good men like my uncle.

There's men want to cut out your eye and pour in bleach.

Most are in between.

Me and Bonnie always said men are going to be men and no program can teach you to change men not even Project Dawn to Dark to Dawn again.

I tell you what. I made a friend in Bonnie Mason. I don't think I ever had a friend before who wasn't a transaction. My way of life did not support that liberty. But when Bonnie lost her girl I could help, and it was not a swap. I wanted her here today, to say Bonnie more than I saved you, you saved me. You made me a person who could be a friend.

Bonnie and Gwen should be here right now and the man cut my eye should be gone. But no one's electing me Jesus any time soon.

Thank you for this program. I'm not a crack whore no more and that is something.

(She goes to sit down.)

JUDGE. Shondell, you're missing a step.

SHONDELL. What?

JUDGE. On behalf of the court, charges seventy-five, seventy-three and forty-nine for Ms. Shondell Bridges shall be dropped with prejudice.
Any objections?

(Nothing. She hits her gavel.)

Charges are dropped.

*(**SHONDELL** is stunned.)*

SHONDELL. I forgot that part. I have a clean record?

JUDGE. You have a record, but you do not owe the state any time for current or prior violations, nor do you owe us parole. In one year, with no new arrests, your record disappears.

SHONDELL. Okay! Okay that's something. Okay!
I won't be seeing you again.

RUTH. We welcome you back any time. To observe and inspire.

SHONDELL. Oh I don't think so.

JUDGE. Well we wish you the best with your grandchildren, and we are proud of you.

SHONDELL. I'm proud of me too.
I'm gonna take a selfie. Will you be in my selfie, Judge?

JUDGE. I would be honored.

SHONDELL. Ms. Bailiff don't call me out on my phone. I'm an observer now!

BAILIFF'S VOICE. You go on, Ms. Bridges. *Not you, Palladino!*

TRACY. I wanna treasure the moment.

*(**SHONDELL** poses with the **JUDGE**. A selfie.)*

SHONDELL. Oh my god oh my god oh my lord I have finished. Do I have to sit through the rest of the day?

JUDGE. You are not obligated, but –

SHONDELL. See you girls later.
Tell Gwen I miss her.
I'm staying clean. I'm doing it for my girl Bonnie wherever she may be.

JUDGE. Do it for yourself.

SHONDELL. I know, it's a selfish program. And that's okay because I am a selfish person.

JUDGE. Let's take five, to celebrate.

(Sidebar light.)

(Urgent.) We can't proceed without Gwen. Where the hell is she?

NIA. I have a text last night, then nothing. I am calling all her numbers.

NOELLE. I have the binder, I'm confident filling in.

KYLA. You are not the understudy. You don't go on.

NOELLE. I have a 171 LSAT.

KYLA. That is an aptitude test, and a flawed one, suggesting you have the aptitude, *after* legal training and the bar, to serve as a lawyer.

JUDGE. Nia, where are we with backup?

NIA. *(On phone.)* We are waiting on a relief lawyer from the Public Defender's office; they're all in court until one.

KYLA. Let's adjourn until one.

JUDGE. I have a conflict.

RUTH. Has anyone heard from Joe? Or the children?

NIA. The younger kids are with her sister.

KYLA. The crazy one?

NIA. Is there another one?

KYLA. What are we going to do without Gwen?

NIA. She has been asking for a replacement.

JUDGE. I heard from the mayor yesterday. He has not "seen sufficient gains to justify a dedicated hire." There will be no replacement.

KYLA. Dammit!

NOELLE. I applied for a grant to keep the court running. Matching funds.

KYLA. Matching what funds?

NOELLE. Whatever's our budget.

NIA. Do you see my shopping closet? And my little soaps and shampoos?

NOELLE. Yes.

NIA. Everyone in the court building donates. Cops, lawyers, security guys. Stay in a hotel, bring us the shampoo, so the girls can wash their hair.

NOELLE. I assumed there was –

NIA. We have no budget. Nada.

(Makes a little zero finger sign.)

Zero budget.

JUDGE. Except for Nia.

NIA. That's right. My massive millionaire-ita salary is the only expense of Project Dawn Court. I am the single paid employee.

NOELLE. I'm gonna crowdsource this thing.

NIA. Do you have rich parents?

NOELLE. No I have a lot of loans.

KYLA. There is no court without Gwen.

*(**GWEN** enters, rowdy drunk and disheveled. End of sidebar. **RUTH** and **KYLA** move toward **GWEN** to comfort her but also to contain her.)*

RUTH. Gwen.

GWEN. *(To **NOELLE**, too loud.)* HELLO, ROCKSTAR!

KYLA. What happened to you?

GWEN. SHONDELL GRADUATE?

RUTH. She sure did.

GWEN. FANTASTIC.

JUDGE. Gwen may I see you in my chambers?

NIA. We're going to continue sidebar, ladies. Stay in place. No phones. *No phones.*

(Sidebar light.)

JUDGE. I believe you've been drinking.

GWEN. "I don't need to drink a bottle of wine to go to work." Well THAT DAY ARRIVED!

JUDGE. You didn't find Meredith.

GWEN. I found Meredith.

RUTH. Praise God.

GWEN. Don't start with me and God, I swear.

KYLA. Is she safe?

GWEN. She's with Joe! She prefers his company! And since he's leaving me, she can be with him all the time.

KYLA. Oh, Gwen.

GWEN. Apparently Gwen is aggressive! And scary! And yells too much for a cuddly mommy!

Gwen forgot bake sales and lost baby teeth and whatever the fuck else and now Gwen will have to defend her right to custody of the other three. How's it hanging for you all?

RUTH. Kids are rotten.

JUDGE. Ours was a nightmare, for a time.

GWEN. My kids got veggies and gymnastics and stuffies and camp. Fuck 'em.

I am served a poorly worded brief stating I'm a career woman? That I don't care about motherhood? *Fuck them*. If I didn't care about motherhood I would have had abortions, am I right?

JUDGE. Gwen. I respect your contributions to this court.

GWEN. Thank you, Judge.

JUDGE. We would not be here without you.

GWEN. Cheers to me.

JUDGE. And I will do what I can to help you secure custody.

GWEN. Little fuckers.

JUDGE. But you need to leave the court.

GWEN. You wanna give me a urine?

KYLA. Don't go there please.

RUTH. You have permission to be angry, to be frustrated, to be tired.

GWEN. You want to mandate therapy? Lock me up?

JUDGE. We all get stuck with crummy circumstances sometimes.

GWEN. Do we? What were your circumstances, Judge *Kaplan*?

KYLA. Gwen, stand down.

GWEN. **Why is everyone so fragile?** Me me me. My anxiety my anxiety my anxiety. Guess what, there's no pill that makes the world safe. It ain't safe. So shut up and stop wasting my insurance deductible!

JUDGE. Nia, can you escort Gwen?

GWEN. I'm practicing Justice. I'm administering Justice.

KYLA. The girls can hear you.

> (**GWEN** *turns to the court. Sidebar light goes away, indicating that everyone can hear her.*)

GWEN. I AM JUSTICE.

I know right from wrong which is why I started this court.

By now I know when a girl's lying. I know when she's lying but we should help her anyway. I don't need the law. I have my gut and my gut is good.

JUDGE. We adjourn for five minutes, to celebrate Shondell's graduation.

> *(No one moves.)*

GWEN. What are you looking at? Go smoke in the bathroom. We know you do it. You stare at us when we come in there like, "Whatcha gonna do? You founded an entire court to keep me out of jail, you're gonna cite me for *smoking*?"

When Cassie's shelter caught fire, she called her mom, *Mom take me in*. Her mom never took her in from shit, in fact the opposite, but when the roof burns Cassie calls her mom. Now maybe Cassie's a moron. But how come Cassie calls her mom and my daughter left me?

Because I *drink*? When did it become illegal to have some wine in one's own home or occasionally place of business?

Because I'm *strict*? Because I took her effing cell phone when she was texting too late?

Because I'm *interested*? Because *once* I read her texts, traced her contacts, identified delinquent peers, hacked their phones and set up alerts to know when she was near them?

Okay that was disrespectful of boundaries.

But also, *fuck boundaries*. This job is not even my job. So if I was a dot the Ts cross the Is kind of gal you'd all be third floor, no Project Dawn.

Did Jesus have boundaries? No, Jesus did not wait on paperwork which is what separated him from the Jews! He said love. Not law. Love.

RUTH. Gwen. For the ladies.

GWEN. I should have married Jesus instead of messing around with Joe.

KYLA. Where is Joe?

GWEN. You gonna hunt him down? Karate chop his head?

KYLA. I would.

GWEN. Thank you Shondell.

KYLA. I am Kyla.

GWEN. Thank you.

KYLA. Your Honor, we can't continue without a competent PD. I'm going down to the third floor.

(She exits.)

GWEN. I missed Shondell. Three years together and I missed Shondell. Was she good?

NOELLE. She was great.

*(**SHONDELL** appears in the doorway [quick shift from **KYLA**].)*

SHONDELL. You back, Gwen? I thought I heard you.

GWEN. Congratulations, Shondell.

SHONDELL. I'm free. I'm clean.

GWEN. Enjoy your life.

SHONDELL. Gwen, where's Bonnie?

(Beat.)

SHONDELL. I need to know.

GWEN. Bonnie died, on the Ave, where we left her.

SHONDELL. No.

GWEN. Yes.

SHONDELL. You stood by Bonnie, you saw Bonnie, then you *left Bonnie*?

GWEN. Yes.

SHONDELL. No. No.

>   *(She closes the door, exiting.)*

JUDGE. We are adjourned for today. We will all meet at the interim session. Subpoenas for two weeks, everybody.

>   *(**JUDGE**'s gavel. Big protests.)*

TRACY. Two *weeks*? That's for girls with sanctions. We are compliant.

KRYSTAL. I gotta work.

TRACY. Work ain't a priority in this program.

KRYSTAL. Then how I'm gonna pay my security? I gotta get my own place. Who's everybody telling me work ain't a priority?

TRACY. They don't want you to have money girl, they know what we do when we get our money.

KRYSTAL. I do what I do when I *don't* get my money so where does that leave that?

TRACY. Your Honor, we didn't do nothing to get called back at two weeks. It's an undue burden.

KRYSTAL. I start phase four this month, you didn't even announce me. My uncle gets evicted Monday, and I need housing support. This ain't consistent.

JUDGE. You are right. It's inconsistent.

Pick up your subpoenas. I will see you in two weeks.

>   *(**JUDGE**'s gavel.)*
>
>   *(Two weeks later:)*

BAILIFF'S VOICE. March 24, Interim Court.

(GWEN stands with TRACY. GWEN reads from the binder, the first time she has needed her notes. KRYSTAL as a client. NIA and KYLA as staff.)

GWEN. Your Honor, this is Ms. Tracy Palladino. Tracy seems to have straightened out the situation with her sister and secured her own apartment. We haven't done a home visit but it's a nice part of town.

TRACY. Broad and Chestnut, the Morgan building.

JUDGE. That's a very nice building.

TRACY. Business is up.

JUDGE. This is your tattoo business?

TRACY. Everybody wants my art.

JUDGE. Wonderful.

TRACY. I am living in a decent place, Your Honor. No one putting a gun to my head tonight.

JUDGE. Nia do you have Tracy's rental application on file?

NIA. No Your Honor, I do not.

TRACY. Because the court did not have an apartment for Tracy. The Morgan building has an apartment for Tracy.

JUDGE. Congratulations Tracy on what I'm sure is a beautiful home. I just wonder if the landlord would have needed to see some kind of income verification?

TRACY. They trust me.

KYLA. This is Philly.

TRACY. I'm helping out my friend while he's away, covering some rent. I take care of things.

KYLA. What things?

TRACY. I water plants.

KYLA. How often?

TRACY. What?

KYLA. How often do you water the plants?

TRACY. Twice a day. I'm very responsible.

KYLA. You can't water plants twice a day, they'll rot.

JUDGE. Nia, do you have this address on file?

NIA. No Your Honor I do not.

KYLA. Check activity under the sister's name as well, please.

NIA. In process.

TRACY. That is paranoia right there! Paranoia and distrust in man's ability to reform.

JUDGE. Tracy. One goal of the Project Dawn Court is moving towards independence.

TRACY. Done and done done.

JUDGE. And in most cases, clients exiting our program do not have the means to rent an apartment at all, let alone in the Morgan building.

TRACY. I am exceptional.

JUDGE. Nonetheless.

TRACY. It's just a one-bedroom, Your Honor. Courtyard facing not the river view.

JUDGE. I see.

TRACY. My friend gave me a deal. And my art is popular.

(A new tattoo.)

You see this star? Because I am a star, Your Honor. I am the One That Shines. Mayor's giving a dinner for former prostitutes and guess who got an invite? Palladino. You ought to see my dress.

JUDGE. You will need to show Nia a lease.

TRACY. I told you it's a friend.

NIA. You may present a note from the friend outlining the terms of your sublet, as well as a copy of his lease or mortgage.

TRACY. I got a place where my son can sleep; I got an elevator.

KYLA. Nia, check vehicles, shipping, bank accounts, and loans under both names.

NIA. *(Off her research.)* Tracy. We're gonna meet.

TRACY. Does my lawyer have anything to contribute?

GWEN. Nuh-uh.

TRACY. Can you speak in my defense or are you tanked again?

GWEN. Neither.

TRACY. I'm being profiled for my work ethic. I am industrious. I am a powerful woman with a powerful mind.

KYLA. Yes, and every one of the eighteen times you went to jail your powerful mind got you there.

TRACY. I am very disappointed in my country.

(NIA escorts ASHLEE in from the side door. ASHLEE wears handcuffs. Very low affect.)

KYLA. Gwen you okay?

(GWEN stands hurriedly.)

GWEN. Your Honor this is Miss Ashlee Fuller. She has been brought to court in custody; she has two weeks left of her sixty-day sentence.

JUDGE. How are you Ashlee?

ASHLEE. I'm okay. I thought maybe Gwen would visit me, but Ruth came.

JUDGE. Anything to report, Ruth?

RUTH. I think it's been calm for Ashlee.

ASHLEE. It's pretty boring.

JUDGE. We'll take boring.

ASHLEE. Ruth says I have a power spark? A place in me that is strong and helped me survive that shit. But I couldn't really think of what it was.

JUDGE. Any guesses?

ASHLEE. I remembered the man who rescued me? I just saw Pennsylvania plates and jumped in his car, said I'll do anything no charge, please take me to Philly. He didn't speak good English he was from India or someplace he drove me three hours, home. He was one good person.

RUTH. That's him. What about you?

ASHLEE. Well sitting in that boring-ass jail it did occur to me – He was out looking for a trick, but then he didn't touch me, gave me fifty bucks. Why? What did he see up close? He probably looked at me and saw, you know, a kid. Just a dumbass kid. And maybe whatever he saw, in me, that made him change his intent, is my spark.

JUDGE. That sounds very possible.

ASHLEE. I mean probably not. But.

JUDGE. I'll see you in April.

ASHLEE. Am I still in the court?

KYLA. Yes Ashlee, you are.

ASHLEE. Thank you.

JUDGE. Sit with Nia.

ASHLEE. Thank you.

>*(She sits. **RUTH** changes to **KRYSTAL**.)*

GWEN. Your Honor this is Ms. Krystal Williams.

>*(**KRYSTAL** stands, with head scarf, buoyant to the point of manic.)*

JUDGE. Krystal. Good to see you.

KRYSTAL. Great to be here Judge!

GWEN. Krystal has been steady for several months now. Two weeks ago we were ready for an excellent report.

JUDGE. Great, let's pick up from there.

KRYSTAL. Ruth was telling me how people of faith are called to the work you all do!

JUDGE. She was.

KRYSTAL. Now I realize my God calls me too.

JUDGE. Oh.

KRYSTAL. The men have the more sinful actions but we women have sinful natures. My God called me out of those ways and I am proud to be on a more virtuous path. I am so proud and so happy!

JUDGE. I see.

KRYSTAL. He called to me when I was on the chair at three a.m. the third night there weren't no beds at the shelter – he called Krystal, you stay the path, you stay the path and I will uplift you and lay you out on some silk.

JUDGE. Can we back up a minute? Shelter? Chair?

NIA. The uncle's building closed down, and our last court got interrupted so we didn't update Krystal's housing.

JUDGE. You are sleeping in a chair?

NIA. She's on a wait list for a bed at Chances but it's backlogged.

JUDGE. How many people in chairs?

KRYSTAL. Maybe forty, forty-eight?

JUDGE. You are sleeping in a chair in a room with fifty people.

TRACY. And you're on me for my *apartment*!

JUDGE. *(From notes.)* I'm looking at your psychiatric / history –

KRYSTAL. I thought I was schizophrenic but it's God's voice!

JUDGE. Allah is talking to you in the chair? I don't like this.

KRYSTAL. Sometimes He is in the chair, sometimes He is the chair, sometimes He is the lady next chair down.

JUDGE. Nia, if you explain the delusions can she get priority?

NIA. *(From phone.)* Delusions are good. I'm working that.

KRYSTAL. Not delusions! I am clear in my mind! They have me speaking at Step Ahead!

JUDGE. Krystal we are proud of you, we want to support your mental stability.

TRACY. They'll get you a damn bed, but rise up past that they will slam you back down. They will audit your ass.

KYLA. When was Krystal's last urine?

NIA. A week ago.

KYLA. Did the antipsychotic show up?

NIA. Yeah, but a week is a long time if you're homeless.

KYLA. Krystal, do you take your medication at the shelter?

KRYSTAL. Ms. Grant you ever hear of Afrocentric theory?

KYLA. Do you even have your medication?

KRYSTAL. What's up is what is suppressed, right? Freud was this dirty old man always talking about sex is what's repressed. But in Afrocentric theory *race* is the unconscious. *Race* is what we don't discuss. And historically our people have been mislabeled and medicalized by the white / system.

KYLA. Be that as it may Krystal, your medication is part of your legal compliance.

KRYSTAL. It is so natural for you to police a black woman's body. Where do I sleep, what's in my pee?

KYLA. I need to support you within the structure of the justice system.

KRYSTAL. The *system* is crazy. Not me.

GWEN. We want to help you.

KRYSTAL. You can't unmolest me. You ain't been able to get me off that chair. I need a bed and a shower. You show me that I'm good. Otherwise I quit.

KYLA. You can't quit.

KRYSTAL. I do quit.

KYLA. You pleaded no contest.

KRYSTAL. What's that?

KYLA. You gave up your right to a trial. Krystal, we went over this many times.

KRYSTAL. I don't recollect it.

KYLA. If you break the terms of the program you do the maximum sentence for all charges. With your priors that's four years upstate.

TRACY. Are you shitting me? For *hooking*?

KRYSTAL. I didn't break the terms. I'm just done.

KYLA. That's the deal Gwen and I made with the people of Pennsylvania to start this court and to justify its continued use of resources.

KRYSTAL. I ain't seeing no resources. I ain't even seen no breakfast. Resources.

KYLA. You are accountable for your choices.

KRYSTAL. But the judge says I'm crazy, so how can I be accountable?

TRACY. Good question.

KRYSTAL. If I'm not accountable just give me a bed and something to eat. And if I *am* accountable don't get between me and my God.

(She walks toward the door.)

KYLA. You are under subpoena. This is not a visit. This is a court.

*(**KRYSTAL** keeps walking.)*

Stop where you are.

*(**KRYSTAL** keeps walking.)*

*(To **BAILIFF**.)* Take her into custody.

KRYSTAL. DON'T TOUCH ME!

(But she stops.)

KYLA. Sidebar!

KRYSTAL. You sidebar I'm gonna walk and you're gonna throw a homeless black lady in prison! That your power?

*(**KYLA** stays controlled.)*

KYLA. Krystal. Any power I hold is not mine but society's. I play a role in this court right now, and you play a role in this court right now. You may not like your role and I may not always like my role but **let's do our jobs now Krystal**.

I am going to sidebar to speak to my colleagues. Do we need to use restraints?

KRYSTAL. Don't shackle me! I'll wait.

(She returns to the stand. Sidebar light.)

KYLA. We screen for mental illness and you give me this?

GWEN. Krystal was stable on her meds. You didn't want to exclude her from this court.

KYLA. I am calling for restraints in Project Dawn Court!

GWEN. I could start the procedure to question competency.

NIA. That's a thirty-day process at least.

KYLA. I became a prosecutor to get the bad guy. Krystal is not the bad guy.

GWEN. Work within the law. Isn't that your philosophy?

KYLA. At one time slavery was the law.

NIA. Maybe Krystal truly is seeing God. People at my house talked to God all the time.

JUDGE. So Krystal is fine and we have a cultural misinterpretation?

GWEN. Krystal is not fine. She is homeless sleeping on a chair.

KYLA. She reached phase four of the program and *now* threatens to quit, which a hundred percent undermines her own interest.

GWEN. Plus if she starts seeing God too close in the gal on the next chair, she's gonna get her ass kicked.

KYLA. How can she pursue long-term goals without food, sleep, medication, and security today?

JUDGE. You participate in a justice system that separates social entitlements from personal responsibility.

KYLA. Personal responsibility starts to look like neo-libertarian bullshit.

What is a person?

NIA. Pardon?

KYLA. A girl who's been sold since the age of six? No education, *continuous* traumatic stress disorder – there is no "post" – addiction by early adolescence, HIV, diabetes, deep deep poverty. Down to brain chemistry warped by poor nutrition, low verbal exposure, childhood trauma, long-term heavy psychopharmaceuticals, and survival-level desperation.

Is that a person or an animal?

GWEN. Kyla, I'm shocked.

KYLA. Krystal has less than what she needs to survive as an animal: no shelter.

NIA. I'm finding her something.

KYLA. For a night.

NIA. There's Section 8.

KYLA. With a criminal record you don't get Section 8.

NIA. The court expunges the record if she completes the program.

KYLA. How is she going to complete our helpful but time-consuming program without housing? We focus on the individual not the system, tell our clients to "re" cover when they were never covered in this world.

I entered recovery at twenty-two; I got a career, a wife, a house. Krystal stays out of the life, she's still on the plastic chair. Of course she can't set long-term goals. My whole work is backwards.

If Krystal walks for that door, I must call in the cops, deliver her to prison, lock up an individual who has been a leader in this program, but succumbed to homelessness and a medical condition. Where is the order in that?

GWEN. I give up too.

KYLA. Whoa whoa whoa whoa that's not what I meant. I am questioning our efficacy. I am raising our game.

GWEN. I have been meaning to talk to you Kyla. Now's not the right time.

KYLA. Now is a brilliant time.

GWEN. No, you're saying your theory. Go on.

KYLA. Go *on*? You go on. You don't give up, you get up. You run this court with Kyla. We will break this cycle. We will show those bros at City Hall. We will triumph.

GWEN. You triumph.

KYLA. What is occurring?

GWEN. Noelle got the grant.

NIA. What grant?

KYLA. Gwen you're my partner in justice. We're going to fix this.

GWEN. I've been telling you every day I need a replacement.

KYLA. That's just shit nonprofit people say.

GWEN. No Kyla.

KYLA. You took a hard lesson in self-care. This is a wake-up call. You just need to reapproach, rebalance.

GWEN. Stage two gets you a Johns Court.

KYLA. What are these words?

GWEN. Stage one of Noelle's grant funds a replacement lawyer.

KYLA. What lawyer?

GWEN. She starts Rutgers in the fall.

KYLA. That makes her a law student.

GWEN. She'll study nights. I'll supervise.

KYLA. Your Honor?

JUDGE. Apparently Noelle has secured a generous grant that will fund her salary for two years. Like an internship.

KYLA. This is not entry-level law.

JUDGE. I wish I had funding to keep a veteran like Gwen, but the state has nothing. The city has nothing. Yet I believe in the court and I think you do too.

(**TRACY** *is impatient.*)

NIA. We will pick up in a minute, ladies.

(*Sidebar light.* **ASHLEE**, **KRYSTAL**, *and* **TRACY**.)

ASHLEE. Every time it's my turn they sidebar.

KRYSTAL. It ain't your turn, strawberry shortcake. It's still my turn.

ASHLEE. Fuck you. I want them to be proud of me.

TRACY. Fuck all you girls I got some plants to water.

ASHLEE. I'm going to tell what you're selling in that apartment.

TRACY. You ain't invited up.

KRYSTAL. Morgan building. Where is that?

TRACY. Center City, you don't know Center City?

KRYSTAL. Why would I go there?

TRACY. Because it's the center. Of the motherfucking city.

KRYSTAL. Morgan building.

TRACY. I can hear them in sidebar.

ASHLEE. What you're a superhero now?

TRACY. Super hear-er. Yeah it's a gift.

ASHLEE. You piss me off. You ain't better.

TRACY. I'm a success.

KRYSTAL. You should be in prison.

TRACY. I'm an entrepreneur.
KRYSTAL. Don't make me mad.
TRACY. You want to know what they're saying?
ASHLEE. No.
TRACY. Useless. Hopeless. No repair. Toss 'em out like trash.
ASHLEE. They see us as precious and worth protecting, asshole.

(In sidebar light.)

KYLA. Gwen. Stay in this with me. It's a mess but it's our mess.
GWEN. I am bone-tired.
KYLA. Inject B-12.
GWEN. I came to court drunk.
KYLA. We're all about second chances.
GWEN. I signed up for a sprint that turned into a marathon.
KYLA. Take a week to rest.
GWEN. Kyla. I need to get my kids back.
KYLA. You know that's sexist bullshit to punish you for working.
GWEN. Yeah but I need those little fuckers back in my house. I maybe don't want to drink that bottle of wine a night. You've been there.
KYLA. Long time ago.
GWEN. How did you stop?
KYLA. I changed everything.
GWEN. Kyla. I need help.

*(**KYLA** takes this in.)*

KYLA. *(To the **JUDGE**.)* What's this business about a Johns Court?

*(**NOELLE** emerges from **ASHLEE**. **KYLA** barely acknowledges her presence.)*

NOELLE. Stage two of the grant. We can collect names now, and start in six months.
KYLA. Can you speed that up?

NOELLE. I can try.

KYLA. Your Honor what about when this grant runs out?

JUDGE. It's an interim solution.

KYLA. The women deserve better.

JUDGE. All this court has ever been is an interim solution.

KYLA. We need to prosecute the men.

NOELLE. In Sweden it's illegal to pay for sex or to sell someone else for sex but not illegal to sell your own body for sex. Isn't that a good idea?

KYLA. Meanwhile, in Philadelphia.

NOELLE. I'm all about local.

KYLA. We need to change the pattern of bookings, sting the buyers. If that means more women cops, hire more women cops. If we insist on accountability let's make the numbers fair.

JUDGE. That would be the goal.

KYLA. Now a Johns Court is something Harrisburg could not ignore. That is a cultural shift that could change the game. Because the johns are the ones with more to lose. They have jobs, kids, wives; they don't want their picture in the paper.

NOELLE. Picture in the paper, great idea.

KYLA. This could be national.

NOELLE. That's right. We're a team.

KYLA. Maybe. Eventually. But we are also opposing counsel, so you'd better prepare.

NOELLE. Yes sir.

JUDGE. Where are we with Krystal?

NIA. Holding for a bed.

JUDGE. Keep holding. Who's next?

GWEN. Lola, Your Honor.

KYLA. Lola?

GWEN. Lola made it home.

KYLA. Well I'll be damned.

(End of sidebar. **GWEN** *hands* **NOELLE** *the binder.* **NOELLE** *stands with* **LOLA**.*)*

NOELLE. Your Honor, this is Ms. Lola Vargas. She returned from San Diego last week as promised. She was able to keep up with her studies and resume her job.

JUDGE. I'm glad to see you.

LOLA. Me too, Your Honor.

JUDGE. Will you tell us about your trip?

LOLA. Yes I will, Your Honor.

I tied my coat to my suitcase by the arms and didn't put it on one time in nine days.

It's not hot like summer, that's how I thought it was in California, summer in the winter.

It isn't summer. It's bright and, I guess you'd call it mild. It's mild.

The plane lands right by the water, it lands like through palm trees like the plane on Fantasy Island, if you're old like me you remember, Da Plane, Da Plane, but I was on the plane. That was cool.

My moms got old but she's smiley. Her boyfriend's nice. They drink beers in the garden. The complex has a lemon tree. It's like a little bit of heaven landing there.

Her boyfriend Manuel picked me up. She was waiting in the car. That confused me because I came to see her not him, but she waited.

She's always afraid.

Mom she was always afraid of everything. She's a good person but I mean, you that scared how good can you be? How good can you do?

Also she was watching the car at the curb so they didn't have to pay no parking fees.

Everyone speaking Spanish in San Diego, everybody, more even than Philly, but Mexican, they sound all beaner.

When I got on the plane, a white baby was in my seat. I saw from three rows away and my heart was pounding because Nia printed out my ticket and I know my seat number by heart so I'm thinking holy lord what if I can't fly after all? I get to my row and I just stand; the man and lady have these vests not exactly matching but like they went to the same store, him and her? And he's wearing this ugly fabric pouch.

So he looks at her like, you say it, and she's like, "Oh our seats are over in that row but we want to be together in this row where there's room for the baby so could you do 22C instead of 18A, it's an Aisle." And my mom bought my window seat two months ago so I could see where I'm going.

My stomach starts chopping up and I'm sweating in my coat, and she's looking at me like I'm, not dirt more like a rock in the middle of a road she's walking, oh what is this obstacle? And she's like, "Do you have kids?" and I'm like, "Yes ma'am I do." And she's like, "You know how it is."

And I feel good that she can't tell what I am, but also I want to say, "Actually this is my first plane ride and my son's in jail and my other son's in the army and I'm proud of him but also scared for him and I'm fighting for my daughter, and I gave up three more, I gave up three more, and none of those kids ever went on a plane with me so I don't know the particular problem you're describing."

Her baby is screaming and the husband looks pretty useless with the pouch. She shows me on her phone screen, the 22C, she didn't even put it on paper, and I start to head down. I'm shuffling past 18 to 19, 20, they do cram the people in there, it's like a long line but you're not sure for what? And it smells like a bathroom, a clean bathroom but those solvents?

And I think the word: "No."

(Lights focus on her.)

And I stop.

And I turn around, which is not easy because the aisle is built for little stick people, and I say to the person behind me excuse me I need to go back. I'm carrying this big bag because it costs thirty dollars for them to take my bag, and all the storage is gone because, I'm not sure maybe people put the bags over other seats that aren't theirs?

But I get back to 18A and I say, "I would like to sit in my own seat."

And they go sure, sure, but she's side-eyeing me. And I just look straight ahead pleasant, like I don't need to throw shade, I got the seat. I have my paper.

And I wait patiently while he packs the baby back into the pouch and she gathers the damn cut-up fruit into little boxes and he unlocks the baby seat and she folds the iPads and they just take you know a very long time shuffling back to the two not three seats they paid for, in the row where they belong.

And I removed my coat, and leaned on that window, and passed six hours in bliss.

And by the time I met my mom she could disappoint me again. Because I did not disappoint me.

I forgave everyone, even the ones that didn't ask.

Thank you, Your Honor, for the opportunity.

I had a true vacation.

End of Play

Thoughts on Ruth's Writing Workshop

Ideally, the audience will experience this workshop along with the characters, writing or at least thinking about their own answers to Ruth's questions. You can distribute paper and pencils at intermission and make clear the answers are private. Some variables that may or may not allow the writing to happen include:

The vibe of your theater and its audience – are they game for participation or more cautious?

The setup of the stage/court – is the audience already included, so that it's relatively easy to keep the house lights up and feel part of Ruth's workshop?

If you cast a live Bailiff in the show there is more to watch onstage and the audience will be less likely to look away to do their own writing.

While it would be really interesting for this to be a real-time writing exercise, if you can't get your audience to do it, please don't set them up to fail! Just let the scene play out and compress the timing a bit. Ruth might project the following questions one at a time on a screen, which the audience can ponder too. Or you might include a handout like this one on the program, for audience members to consider on their own time:

Ruth's Workshop
A USER'S GUIDE TO POWER
Inspired by Vanessa Jackson, LCSW

These questions are yours to answer privately, discuss, or ponder

1) What is your working definition of power?

2) How does this definition of power shape your experience of being powerful or powerless?

3) Think back to an early time when you felt powerful. How, if at all, does this event influence your life today?

4) Think back to a time when you felt powerless. How, if at all, does this event influence your life today?

www.ingramcontent.com/pod-product-compliance
Lightning Source LLC
Chambersburg PA
CBHW051409290426
44108CB00015B/2211